# The Magic of the Seal

## Ocean Messengers

# What people are saying about

# The Magic of the Seal

If you are drawn to explore the rich myths and legends about these soulful beings; to honour them in your spiritual practice and to help in their protection and preservation, *The Magic of the Seal* is a great place to start. With fascinating folklore and practical suggestions to build your own bonds with these magical creatures, Melanie also shares her healing encounters with seals – both in the material world and in her own inner landscape – illustrating their power to guide us back to our truest, most authentic selves, and to help us stay connected with our innate sensitivity, creativity and compassion.
**Philip Carr-Gomm**, author of *Druid Mysteries*

Seals and humanity have had a long and complicated relationship for thousands of years, appearing in our sacred stories and being seen by many peoples in the northern hemisphere as ancestors. In this book, Melanie Godfrey explores the figure of the seal, its lore and relationships to humans, from across the globe. Godfrey explores the seal from both a historical and spiritual lens, offering an intimate and deeply personal journey of relating to these remarkable creatures. Coming from a deep place of love, Godfrey has written an homage and a call to action to the reader. A must read for seal lovers!
**Ben Stimpson**, author of *Ancestral Whispers: A Guide to Building Ancestral Veneration Practices*

A wonderful deep dive into the powerful mythological world of seals, their sensibilities and powers, Melanie's book guides us all through seal history. Seals are healers and a single encounter has led many of us humans through a life changing experience onto an eternal journey to help society to appreciate, care, respect and protect these eternally magical creatures.

**Sue Sayer, MBE**, author of *Seal Secrets: Cornwall and the Isles of Scilly*

Charming, fascinating, and utterly enchanting, Melanie Godfrey's *The Magic of the Seal* opens a secret doorway into the hidden lore and mythology of the seal. Equal parts history, folklore, and practical ways to work with seal magic, Godfrey is a natural storyteller who deftly weaves a tale nearly as old as the sea itself, that of our ongoing interdependent relationship with nature.

**Danielle Blackwood**, author of *The Twelve Faces of the Goddess*, and *A Lantern in the Dark*

*The Magic of the Seal* is a poetic and spiritual exploration of seal magic across belief. Worth reading if you love seals, are drawn to the sea, or find fascination in the magic of these things.

**Morgan Daimler**, author of *Aos Sidhe*, and *Fairy: The Otherworld by Many Names*

# The Magic of the Seal

## Ocean Messengers

Melanie Godfrey

**MOON
BOOKS**
London, UK
Washington, DC, USA

# CollectiveInk

First published by Moon Books, 2024
Moon Books is an imprint of Collective Ink Ltd.,
Unit 11, Shepperton House, 89 Shepperton Road, London, N1 3DF
office@collectiveinkbooks.com
www.collectiveinkbooks.com
www.moon-books.net

For distributor details and how to order please visit the 'Ordering' section on our website.

Text copyright: Melanie Godfrey 2023

ISBN: 978 1 80341 606 9
978 1 80341 623 6 (ebook)
Library of Congress Control Number: 2023941658

A CIP catalogue record for this book is available from the British Library.

Design: Lapiz Digital Services

UK: Printed and bound by CPI Group (UK) Ltd, Croydon, CR0 4YY
Printed in North America by CPI GPS partners

Cover artwork by Leanne Daphne

We operate a distinctive and ethical publishing philosophy in all areas of our business, from our global network of authors to production and worldwide distribution.

# Contents

For Elizabeth and all the wild seals who wander the oceans,
who need our compassion, protection, and understanding.

# Acknowledgements

This book is in honour of Elizabeth and all the seals who inhabit the coastline. Without my encounter with Elizabeth, the graceful Otherworldly seal pup I found at Boscastle Harbour in 2017, this book would not have been written. For she invoked within me a passion to understand her kind.

I'm grateful to: my family for their love, encouragement, and belief in me; Linda Williamson, for her kindness in helping me to understand the truth about seal lore; Sue Sayer, MBE, and founder of the Cornwall Seal Group Research Trust (now Seal Research Trust, a national charity), for her incredible knowledge and passion to protect the UK's rare grey seal; Philip Carr-Gomm, Sue Sayer, Ben Stimpson, Danielle Blackwood, and Morgan Daimler for their sincere endorsements. I'm thankful to my editors Christine McPherson, and Trevor Greenfield and to Moon Books themselves. And finally, I thank those who I reached out to ask for input in this book. Leanne Ta'lki Anawa for the 'Selkie Moon' artwork; Leanne Daphne for the majestic book cover; and the people of the Isle of Lewis and Harris, Berneray, and North Uist, who touched my heart with their thoughtfulness, hospitality, and seal stories.

The Celtic oceans, and the waters of the world are here to be treasured. We seek tranquillity, and solace at the ocean's fronts, and we return to its flow, time after time. The seal calls us home to our first mother – the ocean – reminding us about homecoming, of embracing our wild natures, and that we are born to live free. My heart feels immense love for these gentle beings, and my spirit is led to peace as I remember the song of the ocean, the song of my soul.

*Melanie*

# Introduction

Seals understand the secret language of the ocean. They know when the gods of the sea are whipping up a storm and how to steer clear of the tempest's wrath. They know when it's safe to venture out to fish-filled depths, foraging through seaweed-laced, salty waters, seeking crustaceans and nuzzling the seabed in search of sand eels and benthic, soft-finned fish, unveiling their presence, and thereafter devouring great fish suppers. Seals travel long distances in short periods of time and return to the exact place where they started their journey, as if there were in-built maps under the ocean. Powerful swimmers, ocean's messengers, and wisdom keepers of the sea's mysteries.

Since bygone days, the ocean was seen as a sanctum of transformation, regeneration, and healing. The ocean inspires solace, and fear – it is both serene and perilous, yet folk return to its flow again and again, to live as well as flourish. The ocean is a doorway to the Otherworld where alchemy is woven, and where the legends of the selchie took form. Certain seals have unusual paranormal talents where they shed their silky skins, enabling them to become human on land. They are not so much shapeshifters, but skin shedders, known as therianthropy. The selchie who are the *larger* of the grey seals are one of the most mysterious sea fayeries in the whole of the fayerie kingdom. Lesser seen, they dwell in isolated places.

Seal lore was seen as a type of religion among the crofters of the Outer Hebrides of Scotland, who spent their lives working beside the sea. The seal people tales ran deeper than imagined fayerie world of enchantment and fantasy. The stories told were genuine and are profoundly significant in the present-day world. Humans cannot endure life alone; there needs to be an alliance with all creatures, a common affection for nature not solely for us to survive, but to thrive and come home to ourselves – heart and soul. Our ancestors knew this. They knew about animistic wisdom and had an enlightened connection to nature, for the song of the selchie is the song of our heart's homecoming. This is the magic of the seal.

There are ocean stories of the mermaids – or merrows, as the Celtic folk like to call them – who are half fish, half human; there are the kelpies; the Finfolk; and the mysterious selchie. Seal lore was kept secret, only to be shared within a family or village. Eventually seal legends began to journey to wider communities, and then shared with the world, only to be held gently, as sacred knowledge, in the palms of people's hands. The storytellers, travellers, fishermen, and crofters spoke with such purity it could crack open the hardest of hearts to the truth of life, and the living Godhead that lives within all of nature, seeping into the souls of open-minded folk who listen not only with their ears, but with the great mystery in mind.

This book is written in two parts. Part I focuses on the myths and legends of the selchie of the northern hemisphere of the world: the selchie beginnings, and stories of traditional oral storytellers who were the transmitters and custodians of folklore who keep seal lore alive. I talk about the seal clans in Scotland and Ireland, who had a sophisticated understanding of the relationship between human being and environment. Part II focuses on connecting to the spirit of the seal, its anima, and unique voice. They teach us that life is temporary, and everything we do is temporary. The selchie stories help us to rekindle a relationship with the coastal environments, and when we hear the seal songs echoing in our hearts, we rekindle a relationship with ourselves. I take you on meditations to connect with the seal. The last chapter shares my experience with a three-day old seal pup who I found desperately seeking help at Boscastle harbour in Cornwall. I rescued the pup, and it went on to be rehabilitated at the Cornish Seal Sanctuary, before being released back into the wild.

On the shoreline where aquamarine waters gently ebb and flow, you will find seals basking on emerald and vermillion seaweed-covered rocks, relaxing amidst the liminality of land and sea. They stay in one place for only a short period of time, as they belong to neither. They rest between solitary foraging pursuits, seeming incredibly lazy, as if they spend all their lives relaxing whilst their silky silver fur glistens in sunlight. But seals are misleading, and they are far from idle. Sleeping a minimal six-and-a-half hours a day, these sensitive beings who are elegant in the water and clumsy on land, need rest. They need to lay down their weary heads by sleeping undisturbed, as they are conscientious hunters by day, with some seals hunting at night. They sleep to aid in recovering oxygen levels, on top of restoring body temperature. The seal people are spirited, harmless folk, shy, timid, a little nervous, but who only want to be left in peace to go about their day.

Thirty-three species of *pinnipeds*, which is from a Latin word meaning "fin-footed" and is another term for seals, inhabit our earth today. This book will focus mainly on the seals who occupy the Northern hemisphere of the world, especially the common and rare Atlantic grey seal who thrives on Celtic shores. These placid, semi aquatic, Otherworldly souls are one of the most powerful animal teachers. They bring forth lessons about transformation, and liminal space which we all encounter; they teach us about the deepest of peace, and profound gentleness, and extreme courage and strength. Seals are not ordinary; they are extraordinary, metaphorically teaching us to live beyond the mundane, to live our ultimate truth and beyond.

Seals are Albion's natural treasures and ocean's messengers, bringing valuable evidence of environmental changes to our shorelines. Evidence of oceanic warming and pollution is seen in the seals' stomachs, with increased parasitic growths and entanglement with plastic waste. Seals are messengers of the afterlife and bring hope in times of grief. A belief is held among fishermen and crofters in Ireland, and the islands of Scotland, that folk who have drowned at sea go to live with the seal people, or become one. They are, therefore, our ancestors. Seals and humans are kindred, with their human cries, the tears they shed from compassionate eyes, and their intelligent and curious characters. Is there any wonder our ancestors connected so profoundly to these Otherworldly creatures?

In the not-so-distant past, there were seal clans. The seal clan of North Uist – the MacCodrum of the Seals – and the Conneely clan of West Ireland, who both remain a mystery. Little was documented about these clans, yet, as I went in search of evidence, I found a rich heritage on the lands where the clans originated. Kindly storytellers on the Outer Hebrides told me tales about seals, and before long a story formed in my mind; a story I will share in the coming pages of this book. My heart is forever changed from what I have learnt about these enchanting souls.

Seals are instinctive, confident, and proactive, as they intuitively sense the tidal force, and navigate the ocean. They dance in the rolling waves of the perpetually moving ocean, and have learnt to adapt and survive for millennia through skilfully *knowing* the sea and the forever changing tides. If they did not have an understanding of the ocean's ways, they would be gone. They are in a state of oneness with the world – equal to all marine mammals, animals, and humans alike. Seals possess skills they have fine-tuned throughout the centuries, having individual insight of the world – an insight humans will never truly understand. We are all connected to a subtle energetic web of the earth and live in symbiotic relationship. *We need the seals, as much as they need us.* This book is written to give seals a voice – with goodwill, I hope I have managed to do this.

*Melanie*

# Part I

# The Selchies' Beginnings

There is an old tale from thousands of years ago about the Kiviuq which may have seeded the beginning of the legend of the selchie. These stories spread far and wide around the Arctic Circle, consequently landing on Celtic shores. Dr Andreas Hoffmann, PhD, artistic director of Arctic Culture Lab, Greenland, goes on to share the tale:

> *For the Coastal Sami people of Northern Norway, as for all indigenous peoples of the North, seal is one of the most important natural resources and commodities, a fact which underlines/proves this animal is present in the narrative of the North. The several thousands of years old story of Kiviuq, the eternal Inuit wanderer, starts with a handicapped boy who is abused and mobbed by others. He takes revenge by transforming into a seal, luring his persecutors out on the sea where he creates a storm which kills his tormentors. Even though the boy with power to transform has no name, this epic story of the Inuit finds new ground east of Greenland, on Iceland, the Faroe Islands, Orkney islands, Shetland, where the name Selkie appears.* (Excerpt from a project presentation by Andreas Hoffmann at Arctic Art Summit, Rovaniemi, June 2019.)

Although the story of the Kiviuq may have birthed the selchie stories, it is nevertheless still an enigma where selchie lore originated, and there are many theories. Seals are one of the oldest semi-aquatic mammals on earth, who developed from a carnivorous ancestor who walked on land and later evolved flippers and fins to become ocean dwellers. A walking seal called *Puijila*, who lived in the Arctic Circle around 24 million years ago, was found as a transitional fossil by Natalia Rybczynski at Devon Island, Canada. *Puijila* bears a resemblance to an enormous otter but is a seal. This fossil was thereupon named *Puijila darwini*, which is an Inuit word, meaning young seal.

Mysticism surrounds seals; they are different from land mammals, and with their dreamy eyes, one is transported to another plane of existence. No animal species has ever made me feel the way a seal has. With the field mouse, the great British hare, or the horse, for instance, there is a sense of grounding when you look into their eyes; when you look into the eyes of a seal, it feels Otherworldly.

In the book *The Inner Hebrides and their Legends*, Otta Flora Swire has her own theories where seals originated, and says they were known in the Hebrides as the Pharaoh's army:

> ...*seals they became and seals they have remained. There are, however, certain difficulties over this theory of the seals' origin. Allowing that seals are certainly men and women suffering under enchantment, if they were Pharaoh's army, where do the women come from? Then, some feel that Pharaoh and his men were hardly a pleasant enough people to be the ancestors of our seals. Another trouble is that seals when in human form talk Gaelic and it is unlikely that the Egyptians knew the language, even though it was the tongue spoken by Adam and Eve in Paradise.*

Otta goes on to state:

> *If seals were Egyptians, how do they come to speak it?*

Otta shares more theories of the selchies' origins, stating that:

> *Saint Patrick was responsible. The saint had a fiery Irish temper and, when he preached to the heathen and many were converted, he became very angry indeed with those who were not. If they did not believe, he said, it was the equivalent of calling him a liar, and he turned the unbelievers into seals. St Columba, of gentler*

*nature, saw the difficulties to be overcome, and when St Columba was occupied elsewhere, quite a number of new seals found their way into the sea round Iona. It was mentioned anyone who had been baptised a Christian and relapsed into heathen beliefs were transformed into seals.*

The Finfolk, and the selchie legends found in the Northern hemisphere of the world, were said to be similarly hostile beings. But in recent times, the stories of the selchie became more warm-hearted. Selchie lore is found around Norway, the Faroe Islands, Orkney, Ireland, and the West and North coasts of Scotland. In Scotland, the seal-folk are named selchies or silkies originating from the Scots language called *selch,* meaning grey seal, and is the name I prefer to call these magical beings. In Orkney they are termed selkies, and many people believe the origin of the selchie story originates from Orkney. These stories are entrenched in the land. The old Norse word for seal is *orkn,* and *Orkneyjar,* translates to Seal Island, and in later years was shortened to Orkney. The word selkie originates from the Orcadian language.

On certain islands around the British Isles, there was an opinion that seals and fayeries are interconnected. In the journal *Ulster Folklife, Seal Stories and Belief on Rathlin Island,* author Linda-May Ballard states that one islander from Scotland shared a tale:

*Well, I heard a yarn, it's the time of rebellion in heaven, and they were cast out and some fell on land, and some fell on the sea, and the seal, he's the one that fell into the sea.*

Beyond a shadow of doubt, no one can be certain where the selchie legends began. Our connection to pinnipeds travels back in history to ancient times. Archaeologists unearthed an early prehistoric shell midden on the island of Oronsay in the

Scottish Inner Hebrides in the late 19th century. The bones of a human hand and the bones of a seal flipper were found set side by side. Human hands and pinniped flippers look similar, and it is unique to find remains of each sat next to one another. Found in a humble shell midden, which is essentially an old rubbish dump, and is not a formal burial ground, this could indicate the seal being a food source rather than used in ritual purpose. But the true meaning of their placements is difficult to discern, as middens may have been a place where death rituals were practiced. Could these shell middens be connected to ceremonial practice, and the spirituality of our ancestors?

In the book *The Natural History of Seals*, William Nigel Bonner shares early evidence of man and pinniped interacting,

> *Two beautiful little engravings of seals survive from the Upper Palaeolithic in the Dordogne. Both are so detailed that it is possible to say without doubt that they are grey seals. One drawing found at Duruthy and engraved on a bear's tooth which has been perforated near the root so that it might have been worn as an amulet, shows a grey seal, recognisable from the heavy muzzle. The other drawing, from Mont Gaudier, is much more detailed and amazingly lifelike. It is engraved on a piece of reindeer antler, and this too has been perforated.*

In recent years, a 2,000-year-old seal tooth pendant, with a hole in the top for leather cord was found by the Swandro Orkney Coastal Archaeology Trust, at the Knowe of Swandro, Rousay, in Orkney. This settlement is quickly disappearing, and being worn away by storms, and oceanic currents that batter the Bay of Swandro. It is evident from these sites that humans had an affinity with seals, whether for food consumption or holding them in great esteem by wearing a symbolic necklace. The question remains of what relationship our prehistoric ancestors had with the seals.

# Selchie Bloodlines on Celtic Lands

Seals have strong hind flippers which powerfully move them through the ocean. They have five "toes" and five "fingers", similar to humans, but with added protruding claws. They use these front flippers to guide their way, and their webbed hind flippers propel them through the deep blue sea. There are tales from Scotland about the children of selchies having webbed feet and hands. In olden days, people born with webbed hands and feet would be outstanding swimmers and were unlikely to ever perish in water. A human selchie union was distinguished by the child having a hereditary *selchie paw*. Those with selchie bloodlines exist today, and you may cross paths with an individual on a remote Scottish Island and have a feeling you have met someone *special* – someone with magic in their blood.

Clan origin and family heritage contribute to the selchie legends, and certain families are associated to the seals through bloodlines. The O'Sullivans and O'Flahertys, in West Ireland. The Conneely family of Connemara were descended from the five sons of the seal-woman, from the tale "The Three Daughters of the King of the Sea." The Conneely Clan were a peaceful people, similarly as peaceful as the seals themselves, living in harmony by the seashore collecting fish, seaweed, and shellfish from the ocean. The folk from Cois Fhairrge, a coastal area west of Galway, say there would be terrible luck befall anyone who harmed them. On Conneely land, it was forbidden to injure a seal. Other clans changed their name to Conneely to grant them safety, for it was forbidden to hurt any of the seal clans.

The families related to the seals in Scotland are the Macphees of Colonsay Island and the MacCodrums of North Uist. Now, it is the MacCodrums of North Uist who interest me most. North Uist is an island of remote beauty in the Outer Hebrides of Scotland, and where the weather is dramatic in its appeal. There were legendary connections with the name MacCodrum and its place of origin. Folklore in the Outer Hebrides was influenced by Norwegian settlers who occupied the area for three hundred years.

> *How the MacCodrums came to be associated with the seals, as shown in Mac-a-Leoir's satire and the traditions of North Uist – named as they were, Clann'Ic Odrum nan ron (The MacCodrums of the seals) – is certainly a curious enough point. At any rate it is plain that the seal was, in the legendary lore of the district, connected with the Norse mythology. Griminish, so much associated with Odin, was in olden times entitled to one half of the produce of seal rock of Haskeir, a valuable property in those bygone times.* (Archibald MacDonald, *The Uist Collection: The Poems and Songs of John MacCodrum.*)

The seal hunts of bygone days took place on the rock of Haskeir, and were extremely somber days for the seals. When I visited Benbecula – a steppingstone island between North and South Uist – I met a local diver who told me the Monach Islands, situated near to Haskeir, have the most densely populated area of pinnipeds in the world. When he dived there, he saw hundreds, if not thousands of seals. It is estimated that around 10,000 pinnipeds rest on the Monach Islands every autumn to have their pups. The thought overwhelms my heart. In the olden days, the seal rock of Haskeir was extremely valuable with its connection to Norway and the God Odin, and seal hunts took place every year. But the Clan MacCodrum of North Uist would never join this hunt due to their belief they were related to seals. Today, no hunting takes place at the rock of Haskeir, and the seals live free from harm. I was sure I witnessed a strange luminous glow emanating from the islands as I viewed them from afar.

*The Uist Collection* goes on to express:

> *The connection of the seal with the remains of Norse mythology in Uist is clearly seen in this fact, that at the time of the annual visit to the seal rock — Bualadh na sgeire — a horse racing was held in the district, and there are many still living who remember it, which was called An Odaidh. There can be little doubt that this function was the survival of a Pagan festival in honour of the Scandinavian God Odin, who was so much connected with the district, and that its observance was continued as a propitiation for the slaughter of seals.*

On the island of Uist it was believed the seals were called *Clann righ fo gheasan*, which translates to the children of the Scandinavian King. They were meant to be the king's children who were under enchantment from a witch's spell. Seals were thought to be royalty. *The Uist Collection* explains:

> *The supposition was that Clann Ic Odrum, for some reason or another, were of the kith and kin of the phoca, the children of the Scandinavian King or God, and not improbably they were called originally Clann Odain, afterwards Clann Mhic Odain, which was easily transformed into Mac Odrum. What the reason of this association with the seals can only be a matter for speculation; but it may be accounted for by some old tradition that the MacCodrums were of Norse Extraction.*

Exploring the silent places as I took pilgrimage to the Outer Hebrides, I searched to find a MacCodrum to talk to, asking locals if they knew about seal lore or any MacCodrums who lived on the Islands. My pilgrimage took me on a journey that unearthed more than I expected. An overwhelming peace steadies the heart on the untouched land of North Uist. On writing this book,

I met many individuals who shared seal stories. Yet, some of my questions remain unanswered, questions I'd have wished to ask the great bard *Iain Mac Fhearchair* (John MacCodrum), known as *the seal man*. But instead, I found myself standing before his gravestone at Kilmuir cemetery, in awe and wonder. John was a Scottish Gaelic-speaking bard and seanchaidh, which means bearer of *old lore*. John came from an impoverished background; he was untutored, knowing only his native language of Scottish Gaelic. But it was this language and his exceptional intellect and awareness that made him into one of the most admirable Gaelic bards of his time. He is remembered for his brilliance in poetry and storytelling. Before he passed away, John humbly requested a simple gravestone for himself with no fuss – just a plain rock. In later years, a tall monument gravestone was placed in his honour.

I heard from a local on North Uist that John lived in a humble abode situated beneath Kilmuir cemetery, in the hamlet of Hougharry. He served as an official poet of the Chief of Clan MacDonald of Sleat. The land of North Uist, vast, untouched, and beautifully peace-filled, sings an ancient song. It is a land that holds the soul consciousness of the planet within its core Lewisian gneiss rock. The land restores my weary spirit and is healing balm to my soul.

There is much mystery surrounding the MacCodrum of the seals, and their association of being *related* to seals. John was a MacCodrum of the seals, descended from the seal people. The selchie maiden tale from Berneray conveys that one of John's ancestors had fallen in love with a selchie who was one of the daughters of the Norwegian King – a story I share in the Selchie Maiden chapter. The family MacCodrum possessed dark skin, hair, and eyes very similar to the pinnipeds themselves.

Duncan MacKinnon – or his Scottish Gaelic name, *Donnchadh MacFhionghain* – is a singer and storyteller from the Isle of

Berneray. He welcomed me into his cosy home, and we had tea, ate fruit cake, and recited ghost stories. Duncan recalled a seal story he had been told by a local vet in the 1950s, and how all the seals gathered at a beach on North Uist.

The MacCodrums of Hougharry were meant to come first from the seals, although the MacCodrum name was long extinct since the late eighteen hundreds. The last MacCodrum was buried in Aird a' Mhorain cemetery overlooking the vast Atlantic Ocean, a sacred place on silent land. On his burial day, it seems the locals counted three hundred seals who came to the shore, and whilst songs were sang at the funeral, the seals were crying out, making lots of noises, and they lingered until the body of the last MacCodrum was buried. When the ceremony was over, the seals left the beach mournfully, and they were never seen in that number again. This story has been recounted many times by individual storytellers, and it was spoken in truth. This calls to account the kinship of seals and that they do indeed mourn their dead.

The expression clan originated from the Gaelic word *clanna*, meaning children. The Clan MacCodrum were the *children of the seal*. The clan systems began around 1,000 years before Scotland became sovereign. Sadly, there are no MacCodrum left on Uist. As a result of the Scottish Clearances which took place in the 1700s and 1800s, when it is thought by historian John Prebble, around twenty thousand people emigrated to the American Colonies, the Gaels felt an overwhelming sense of cultural displacement. Sheep superseded Highlanders as industrial farming took over the land.

*And in the Highlands there was a new sound, a placid bleating that was to blot out for ever Keppoch's dying call to his children ... Woe to thee, oh land, the Great Sheep is coming!* (John Prebble, *The Highland Clearances*.)

The Gaels endured incomprehensible social, and financial issues because of the forced clearances. Gaelic traditions were discouraged, and musical instruments were burnt so traditional music would not be played. The school systems prohibited the use of Gaelic speaking language, so the Gaelic children lost their identity and therefore suffered immense shame, and mental distress. The Highland Clearances saw the last of the selchie bloodlines leave for Canada. The indigenous Gaelic clans were about truth, and honour, and many bore *an da shealladh*, which relates to having the two sights – a strong connection to the spirit world, and a belief in seal lore. They beheld unparalleled wisdom about how to care for, and live in harmony with nature, and the seals.

Certain words in Scottish Gaelic cannot translate into English. One of these words is *cianalas* – a word spoken by the indigenous people of the Hebrides after they moved to Canada. *Cianalas* means a sense of belonging to a land, and a yearning for a place that is lost in time. The descendants of the MacCodrums are found in parts of Canada, and are the last remaining *children of the seals*. There is a beach on the Isle of Skye that is now inhabited by many seals, and it is a place where the children who were sent away, once joyfully played.

As we remember the clan of the seals, we are taken to the past where life was lived simply yet navigated with exceptional intellect. The Gaels were far-seeing folk, and connected profoundly to the land. Thinking about the past stirred a well of emotion within me. There is an overwhelming threat to all native peoples and wisdoms throughout the world, and their decimation keeps on happening. I need to make peace in my heart for a culture on the brink of extinction.

Researching the Scottish Clearances, the last of the MacCodrums, and the decline of the Gaelic culture through collective modernisation, evoked a melancholy I found hard to shift. But the seal, in its Otherworldly essence, took me to a place of healing. Their spirit does that if you let them. Seals allow us to dwell in depth of emotion; they navigate a way to inner healing. In their peacefulness, they hold space for reflection and stillness. I realised if something lives in our heart, it does not cease to exist but lives for eternity, like an eternal flame.

Indigenous Celtic culture lives within us. Seal lore and the Scottish Gaelic language, which has shared linguistic roots in ancient Sanskrit, is a part of Scotland's cultural identity. For those who are descended from Europeans, an ancient Gaelic knowledge is a part our ancestry. And for the spiritual treasure we continue to lose, it is necessary to somehow keep the spirit of old alive.

# Seals and the Afterlife

On the remote islands of the British Isles, paranormal occurrences are more likely to materialise with no one around to deter spirit, and their presence becomes brighter and more credible. The spirit world and a belief in magic has always surrounded me. I feel safe in the concept of spirit world existing, and have had many sightings of ghosts throughout my life.

After spending time on the Isle of Lewis, Harris, and Berneray, where people shared seal stories, I travelled to North Uist wearing a MacDonald of Clanranald Ancient tartan stole wrapped around me – a sacred talisman of the society it relates to, and my lucky ritual object. The MacCodrums were families of Clan MacDonald, and their motto was "by land and by sea", similar to the seal, belonging to both land and sea. I walked the land where pure white sandy beaches beheld spirits of the people of the sea. Whilst passing through the Golden Road on the Isle of Harris, I came upon an inlet I choose not to unveil, noticing young seals at play in the ocean while beside them two spirit people manifested. Both walked onto the beach, and within a few seconds they disappeared. I stopped breathing for an instant.

"Did you see that?" I looked towards my friend in awe. We pulled the car into a layby and I jumped out and tiptoed to the edge of the beach. The seals took no notice of me but continued to frolic in the waters. The spirits vanished through the veil of time, but their image lingered in my mind. Having the second sight, I am used to noticing spirit world, but I had never seen the spirit of people floating out of the sea. For a long time after, the land held me in its silence as I watched the adolescent seals revelling in the water.

Imagine living in a remote place on the Outer Hebrides in a cottage by the edge of the ocean, when at night a knock comes to the door, and standing there is the spirit of a person. Did the crofters and fishermen have spirit visits, and is this how some of the seal stories were born? It's common knowledge our Celtic ancestors were second-sighted, and today a lot of the islanders have two sights. Visions of spirit world are fleeting; I never question if spirits are real. I know that as individuals our minds have incredible imaginations that can make up fayerie stories and imagine realms within our creative mind, as we hold ancient wisdom in our cells. I also feel some things are unexplainable and are a part of the great mystery. So, I trust my heart, and know on the Golden Road that day I saw two spirit people walk out of the water. They were the people of the sea.

On Orkney and the German Baltic Island of Rugen, it was believed seals were descended from people who had lost their lives at sea. In grief-stricken minds, people turned to seals for solace and comfort. Seals mourn when a clan member passes away, as witnessed in the passage below; a seal expresses passionate lament. The ballad has been sung by numerous bards on the Outer Hebrides. Father Allen MacDonald collected an early version of the song in 1904. It is about a woman who arrived via ship on the Outer Hebrides, and who was in deep mourning. It's a song which echoes the grief of losing a loved one at sea.

*It is I who saw today the wonder*
*The dark-haired girl with curly hair*
*She went to shore to gather shellfish*
*She sat on a rock and made a start*
*She looked around on every side of her*
*She took the shape of a seal*
*Splitting the waves on every side of her*
*They won't believe me, since I was alone*
*That I did not have more people:*
*A boat crew, with oars and a bilge*

It's not only humans who grieve their lost loved ones. Seals mourn when one of their herd transcends to the Summerland's, as witnessed in the lament below; a seal expresses intense sorrow. This song is from the Isle of Uist, after the slaughter of pinnipeds took place at the rock of Haskeir. One night, an old grandmother seal, who would visit the rock at night, recognised some of her family, by their paws, *spog*. They had been mercilessly slayed. She cried out the lament in Scottish Gaelic and beseeched the rest of her family be treated with more kindness.

*Spog Fionghall, spog Fionghall,*
*Spog Spaidreig, spog Spaidreig,*
*Spog mo chuileinn chaoimh chaidrich.*
(Song from *The Uist Collection*, 1894)

Spirits of the people of the sea are witnessed by people who have "second sight", or "the two sights" – something generally passed through their ancestry. Inherent in all of our natures, second sight is a gift from our ancestors, and it is taken from the ancient Celtic belief in the Otherworld – often spoken about in the old legends and the *Mabinogion* which is a collection of old Welsh tales from two manuscripts from around the fourteenth century and contain four branches with eleven prose stories of profound Celtic folklore and symbolic narratives hidden within them.

The Otherworld is invisible, yet becomes visible to certain sensitive people. The ancient Celtic priesthood of the British Isles were the seers. They saw images in their minds eye which were in the past, the present, and the future, and these visions were discerned. Those who have second sight say it is both a gift and a curse, because they can see things about people they would rather not. "*S e gibht a th' ann – ach's e gibht a th' ann nach toil le duine sam bith.* It's a gift – but a gift that no one wants," according to Lexy Campbell (1894–1986). Second sight is intuitive knowing. It is a feeling in our gut, a primal compass which warns us of danger or tells us to go ahead with something. However, critical thinking is an important component when discerning intuitive messages. Critical thinking opens us up to distortion, because second sight can guide, but it can also mislead us.

Everyone has the ability to connect to their intuitive, and psychic senses. I know of many people who do not work with spirit world yet have seen spirits or apparitions. Many people have witnessed ghosts, and maybe you too have a supernatural story to share.

On the remote islands of the Outer Hebrides and the shores of the west of Ireland, the wild Atlantic Ocean batters the coastline and is a force to be reckoned with. Over the years, shipwrecks and oceanic tragedy would frequently take place. As trauma from losing a loved one at sea overshadowed the hearts of family and friends, village folk created stories about the seal people to help soothe their heartache. Stories about how their lost loved ones had gone to live with the seal people. It was a saving grace to believe they navigate spirits to safety.

Pinnipeds are particularly instinctual, intuitive, and they possibly sense the spirit world. Our ancestors around Ireland and Scotland believed the people who drowned not only went to live with the seals, but became a selchie. And at certain times of the year, these seals would venture on land and shed their silky skins in an act of therianthropy, and return to visit their loved ones on starlit nights, only to disappear before dawn.

There was a belief that people who take their own lives turn into seals. Dr Linda Williamson, who specialises in the lore of Scotland's travelling people, shared a moving true story with me about her late husband, Duncan Williamson, who was a part of the Scottish traveller community. Duncan was a singer and wisdom keeper of folklore. His father's sister, Rachel, was a traveller and skilled storyteller who lived in Tarbert, Loch Fyne in Argyll, at the head of the Kintyre peninsula. There are numerous places named "Tarbert" in the Scottish Highlands and islands, and the word is Scottish Gaelic and means "boat carrying."

Let me circle back to this poignant and emotive story. Duncan and his Aunt Rachel were fond of each other, and she shared many stories with him. Rachel fell deeply in love with a man from the Scottish mainland – oh, what a rare treasure to find true love! However, Rachel's father and family would not let the marriage take place, and it must have been heart-breaking for her to be separated from her sweetheart, and soul mate. Following a failed abduction by her Perthshire fiancé, Rachel committed suicide by drowning herself. People said she went to live with the seal people. During her life, Rachel Williamson told various tales about the seals, and I truly believe the seal folk take care of her in the afterlife, and always will.

In the book *The Works of Fiona MacLeod*, William Sharp shares the legend of the seals in the Rune of Manus MacCodrum. Manus was known as one of the seal people, a part of the MacCodrums of North Uist – children of the seals.

> *"It is I, Manus MacCodrum.*
> *I am telling you that, you, Anndra of my blood,*
> *And you, Neil my grandfather, and you, and you,*
> *And you!*
> *Ay, ay, Manus my name is, Manus MacManus!*
> *It is I myself, and no other,*
> *Your brother, O Seals of the Sea!"*

The seals were more than kin to the folk who lived on the Hebridean islands; more than the Scandinavian King's children in the story of the selchie maiden; more than Otherworldly messengers who whisper of oceanic mysteries, and dance betwixt the waves in moonlight – the seals are kindred in a dance of souls – our beloved, and our family. They *are* you and I – our grandmothers, sisters, aunts, our ancestors. The seal clans felt closer to the Otherworld, because the seal crosses the spiritual veil, as ocean messengers, as messengers of spirit world.

## The Selchie's Grave

In the far north-eastern region of Scotland, in the village of Olrig, Caithness, there is an ancient graveyard where a selchie's grave lies. Through whispers in time, a story was told of a fisherman who found a baby wrapped in a seal skin, abandoned on the beach of Castletown. Gossip spread through the community about this child; gossip that lasted throughout her life. The villagers of Olrig believed she was a selchie. As the pure of heart girl grew older, she began to see things others could not; she had *"an da shealladh"* which, as I have already shared is Scottish Gaelic for "the two sights." This did not help her cause, though, when she proclaimed she witnessed Satan near the rafters of Olrig Kirk. Thereafter she was banished from the village. Yet the girl was plainly no witch and of no danger to the parish.

The selchie girl had one friend in the village. This kindly gentleman saw through the poisonous rumours and believed in her psychic nature, but what a tragic life she led, ignored by her community and sent out into the wilderness alone. The girl later perished giving birth to a child. After her passing to the spirit realm, the selchie girl's body was brought back into the village to be buried in the graveyard at Olrig. Her gravestone, which is a beloved stone, holds water, and has special powers of never drying out, even during hot summer days. The spirit of the girl rests among the old section of graveyard behind the church ruin, near the wall. If you ever visit this Selchie's Grave, remember to take offerings of songs, seashells, and seaweed, and immerse your hands in the waters of the grave, allow your heart's desires to come true, and the magic of the selchie wash over you.

# Animism, Totemism, and Shapeshifting

## Animism

Throughout the centuries, animals have been revered by indigenous peoples for their nature and individual characteristics. Celtic society believed aspects of nature has a spirit, a voice, an interrelationship which can be developed, and that includes a relationship with seals.

How can we, as a culture who are so far removed from its ancestral roots, re-establish a connection to a Celtic spirit that unites us all? This lies in reconnecting the spirit of the land, the spirit of animals, and the spirit of the seals as primal symbolic energies that link with ourselves and humanity's consciousness. When the seal and I began travelling together in a metaphorical sense, in an ever-changing relationship, it became a solid companion, and I have grown with the seal's wisdom. I have learnt about depth of companionship, creativity, accessing vast emotion, safety, and reclamation of my own seal skin. If you feel a connection to them, the relational aspect, and spirit accommodated within the seal – then let them guide you. They teach us about the mystery of transformation which can often feel uncomfortable.

Graham Harvey explains in the book *Animism: Respecting the Living World* (Page xiii): "In reality, there are no individuals. There are only relatives and acts of relating." I want to talk about animism, because this is where the magic of the seal exists – in our ancestors' beliefs about the seals having a spirit. Graham goes on to explain:

*Animists are people who recognise that the world is full of persons, only some of whom are human, and that life is always lived in relationship with others. Animism is lived out in various ways that are all about learning to act respectfully (carefully and constrictively) towards and among other persons. Persons are beings, rather than objects who are animated and social towards others. Animism may involve learning how to recognise who is a person and what is not — because it is always obvious and not all animists agree that everything that exists is alive or personal.*

Graham then talks about being in symbiotic relationship with all beings, saying:

*However, animism is more accurately understood as being concerned with learning how to be a good person in respectful relationships with other persons.* (Graham Harvey, *Animism: Respecting the Living World.*)

*Person,* as said by Graham, can mean human, animal, plant, stone, river, sea; and the person we are looking at here are seals. Yet we do not have to be called an animist to have respect for the seals and their magic, as people naturally connect to nature and understand they are not separate from the whole. This book is about deepening our understanding of the seal and their metaphysical essence.

Animism as an anthropological concept that focuses on the consciousness of a person. Indigenous people hold beliefs around spiritual life; a belief the *spirit* of nature is inherent in all beings. I imagine the indigenous Gaels, and the seal clans of North Uist and West Ireland, held animistic beliefs about the seals. The spirit of the land is a meandering, energetic force which flows within the hills, rocks, beached sand, and the ocean. The ocean symbolically transcends us in flow and movement. Take a moment to unite with the land. Simply *be* in stillness and listen. Gently examine the beauty and raw vulnerability of the wild environment and her animals, recognising the space between you both is limitless and there is no real separation. In our brief communication, Graham Harvey expressed:

*...everything communicates. we need to escape the idea that humans are special or separate. But I also think this means dropping the idea that there is a place called 'nature', or that only the possession of 'souls' or 'spirits' makes beings able to engage with others or makes them or us special. Rocks and trees and seals don't need souls to be worthy of respect or able to give and receive gifts.*

Let us spiral back to the seal, whose intelligence I wish to convey. Imagine a creature that inspires imagination, curiosity, and sensitivity, all the while encouraging you to reclaim your inner freedom. A semi-aquatic mammal that lives both on land and sea, unveiling how to balance life in a metaphorical sense. An anima that proclaims joy and playfulness, as you reclaim your true self's wisdom and your own seal skin. The selchie travels between the Otherworlds, revealing how you too can travel in your mind to limitless awe and wonder. Sincere, and compassionate semi-aquatic beings – powerful in water, yet vulnerable on land. This is the magic of the seal.

## Totemism

The anima of the seal reminds us we are spiritually connected to mammals and animals, a concept explored by Sir Edward Burnett Taylor in 1871. Having a seal as a totem is quite different in a sense, as man is related to an animal protector, akin to an ancestral blood relationship with the seal. Totemism, which is an approach of nineteenth century scholars who used it to describe our ancestors' way of making sense of the world. Both instances of animism and totemism see humans as having a profound connection to seals. Emile Durkheim, who was the founder of the French School of Sociology, stated totemism is ultimately the most basic form of religion. Totems are quite often the focus of ritualistic behaviours among clans, hunters, farmers, harvesters, and crofters, found amongst the indigenous peoples of the world. Totemism blends with other belief systems, such as ancestor worship and animism.

*The original homeland of the term 'totemism' is the north-central Algonquian-speaking area of North America. Much confusion revolves around the meaning of the term 'totem'. In the original published reference to the phenomenon by the English trader John Long, in 1791, totemism clearly refers to an individual tutelary or personal guardian spirit (Long, 1904). In the case of the Ojibwa—dodem referred both to one's fellow patrilineal clan members and to an eponymous animal from which the clan was held to be descended or with which its ancestors were otherwise associated* (Warren, 1957:41-53; Jones, 1970:138). This is an excerpt from the book *Anthropology, History, and American Indians: Essays in Honor of William Curtis Sturtevant*, 'Totemism Reconsidered', Raymond D. Fogelson and Robert A. Brightman, William L. Merrill and Ives Goddard who were the Editors (Page 305).

The discovery of the survival of totemism among the British Isles is described in the book *Totemism in Britain*. The author George Laurence Gomme says:

*Britons and ancient Irish, by which particular nations or tribes were forbidden to kill or eat certain kinds of animals; and goes on to suggest; it seems reasonable to connect the rule of abstaining from certain kinds of food with the superstitious belief that tribes were descendants from the animal, from which their names and crests or badges were derived.*

It is said there was a sincere admiration and a considerable anxiety surrounding a totem. Our ancestors held clear beliefs in seal lore – the stories advised folk not to kill or hurt seals as they could be a relative, or we may come back as one in the next life. The contrasting experiences of both positive and negative a clan may encounter with an animal determines the choice of totem. The clan chief may request the clan honour the entire species – in this case, the seal – and forbid the kinship group from disrespecting any seals. If the law was broken, sickness, misfortune, or even death may occur.

In traditional Scottish beliefs, it's unlucky to have a dead seal in your home, and as a personal preference I would not wish to have any part of the seal in my home. "The dead totem," says James Frazer, "is mourned for and buried like a dead clansman." (From the book *Totemism,* by James George Frazer.)

There is no evidence about how Gaelic seal clans honoured the seal; we can only speculate and use our imaginations to journey back into the past. The totem of the clan would have represented its moral consciousness, and was the underlying power in a society. Durkheim says,

> ...he could not escape the feelings that outside him there are powerful causes which are the source of his characteristic nature, benevolent powers that aid him, and assure him a privileged fate. (Emile Durkheim, *The Elementary Forms of Religious Life,* p220.)

The reason I talk about totemism and the seal is because according to academics in the nineteenth century the seal clans share evidence of totemic survival. If we put two and two together, we can see that seal lore links to a totemic belief system. In the journal *Ulster Folklife, Seal Stories and Belief on Rathlin Island,* author Linda-May Ballard shares:

> The full significance of these facts (of the traditional relationship between Conneelys and seals) may be tested by reference to the conditions laid down by Dr Robertson Smith for the discovery of the survival of totemism among the Semitic races. These conditions are as follows:

1. *The existence of stocks named after plants and animals – such stocks, it is necessary to add, being scattered through many local tribes.*
2. *The prevalence of the conception that the members of the stock are of the blood of the eponym animal.*
3. *The ascription to the totem of a sacred character which may result in its being regarded as the god of the stock, but at any rate makes it to be regarded with veneration, so that, for example, a totem animal is not used as ordinary food. If we find all these things together in the same tribe, the case for totemism is complete.*

1: The Conneely and MacCodrum clan were both named after seals. 2: They transformed into seals, relating to them being descended from seals. 3: No Conneely or MacCodrum could kill or hurt a seal without experiencing negative consequences.

Eleanor Hull, author of *Folklore of the British Isles* states:

*Now, in the Irish case all three of these conditions are found together in the same tribe, the clan Conneely, and it is impossible to overlook the importance of such a discovery. It proves from survivals in folklore that totemistic people once lived in ancient Ireland.*

This *seems* to give the understanding there was once a totemic system in force in the British Isles, but the folklore beliefs told carry much more complexity. While Linda-May Ballard questions the validity of nineteenth century scholars' understandings of the concept of 'totemism', she states,

*If we are to accept the qualifications for totemism expressed by Robertson Smith and applied by Gomme, then we may write 'Q.E.D' after Rathlin material. We have on Rathlin, a full-blown seal totem, and apparently proof that the people of Rathlin have*

*organised themselves totemically (i.e., according to a system of animal cults) since time immemorial.*

Just as Robertson Smith states the three significant indicators of a totemic system, we match these with a series of traditions relating to seals, and therefore arrive at a totemic system!

In contemplating the theories of totemism being connected to the seal clans and traditions throughout Scotland and Ireland, there needs to be a deeper understanding of traditional seal lore and the meaning behind its wisdom. The deeper symbology of seals is a little overlooked by totemic theories, as it considers them to be inferior beliefs when in fact seal lore is indeed a superior belief system amongst islanders, who beheld great intellect, and had a deep connection to the natural world. Claude Levi-Strauss, author of *Totemism* explains,

> *By the bizarre character attributed to it, and which was further exaggerated by the interpretations of ethnographers and the speculations of theorists, totemism served for a time to strengthen the case of those who tried to separate primitive institutions from our own, an effect of which was particularly opportune in the case of religious phenomena, in which comparison had revealed too many obvious affinities. It is the obsession with religious matters which caused totemism to be placed in religion, though separating it as far as possible – by caricaturing it if need be – from so-called civilized religions, for fear that the latter might crumble at its touch.*

An intimate connection existed between seals and people. They were not only a symbol of the people, but a protector, a spirit companion, a relative, a helper, and a friend. This bond penetrated deep into the psychology of the society, not only because of the sacred connection between them both, but because the folk living in the coastal regions lived a fragile life close to the wild oceans; the sea was a matter of life and death. The people turned to the seal for its wisdom. For instance, they were often closely observed to predict weather patterns. If seals were noticed mellowing on the rocks, it was a sign of fair weather on the horizon.

Pinnipeds are not only ocean messengers for global change but messengers from the past, bringing the voices of our ancestors. The seal and man are indeed opposite, but they are also the same, being dependant on each other, and that unites them. The seals wish to live in peace, undisturbed by humankind. They are not so different from you and me. We too wish for peace in our lives. The seal clans were known as being a peaceful folk, and if you ever go walking on the lands of the Outer Hebrides, in North Uist, specifically in the hamlet of Hougharry, you will feel a strong sense of peace in the landscape, where no one bothers anyone, and the sense of community is strong.

Symbolism was paramount to the collective life of the clans, as without symbolism the social unity of a community would disintegrate. The Clan MacCodrum, a family of MacDonald of Clanranald, belonged to the ancestry of seals, and although this clan has disappeared from North Uist, their spirit is strong in the heathered rocks, remote beaches, and in the whispering winds. Just because our ancestors are no longer here to teach us how they lived in unity with nature, and the seal, does not mean we cannot take seals into our hearts, understand their symbolism, and learn to honour all they personify.

The fact seals feature predominantly in old folk tales, and stories about the humanity of seals inspire a deep moral code with people, also needs to be pondered upon. Alexander Martin Freeman in the *Journal of the Folk-Song Society* says that it:

> *...brings us into an immediate contact with the seal of folklore who plays in some Gaelic traditions a part similar to that allotted to the bear in the legends of Norway, Serbia and other countries. Of*

31

*all the animals he is the most human in attributes, and the most
closely connected with the human race.*

In the coming pages of this book, you will begin to see how
seal lore relates to *what we might want to describe as* a totemic
belief system once existing in the British Isles. But you see, our
ancestors had a far more complex, and enlightened bond with
nature, and with the seals. We must not forget *totem* was a word
introduced by nineteenth century scholars. Yet the relationship
between human and pinniped stems back millennia, and our
ancestors' relationship with the seal was far richer than the
fairly modern hypothesis of totemism. The seal being both of
land and sea is a powerful symbol, and throughout time, they
have gained a paranormal position. They were a symbol of the
islanders' relationship with the landscape. Our ancestors saw
themselves not in opposition to nature, but standing in unity
with it, and they understood the dangers of ignoring how to
create a harmonious relationship with nature. The importance
of the seal was an intrinsic part of the people's lives, and in my
opinion, for that reason seals should be regarded not only as
totems, but as sophisticated symbology, who were sacred, and
special.

## Shapeshifting

How does shapeshifting apply to our lives? Selchies transform
from seals to humans by an act called therianthropy, which is the
ability to metamorphosise oneself by shapeshifting. The selchie
has an instant paranormal power that fayerie tales are made of,
but shapeshifting can happen in our everyday lives. Every time
you plant a flower bulb, in time that will transform and bloom
through the art of shapeshifting. It is about transformation,
whether that be instant or unhurried.

The idea of transformation is rooted in Gaelic culture. The
prophetic Druids of the last Celtic Iron Age associated with

Gaelic language and ruled over the tribes in the British Isles. The Druids were masters of shapeshifting and transforming their spiritual bodies at will. Druids had the ability to manifest intense fog over lakes, and oceans and stir significant winds to bewilder their nemeses – all in the name of magic. Druids were the keepers of a cultural identity, as they served communities and the bards created poems through the power of their voices, and kept oral storytelling alive. The Gaels who were the Irish, Scottish, and Manx, understood the language of the natural world and seal lore. There are many tales of individuals transforming into animals in the art of shapeshifting. For instance, the three children in the story of the children of Lir. Aoife, their stepmother magically shapeshifts each child into a swan. In the story of Fear Doirche, he changes the maiden Saar into a fawn. There are seals who take off their skins and transform into humans. The magic of the seal is the magic of transformation and is of the old ways here in the British Isles. The tales of transformation share sacred symbolic wisdom, of how humans and wild animals live together in harmony.

Old lore is a representation of a certain time, and culture. One can often overlook the simple messages within complex mythology, as the old stories are often too intricate to understand. But when we simply translate local folklore; a cultures belief, customs, traditions, and its stories, we can then gain insight into how our ancestors lived their lives, and perceived the *genius loci* of the natural world; this is especially true about seal lore in Ireland and Scotland. We can form a picture in our minds of how our ancestors walked alongside the seal, and what they represented to them. We can take what that means for us in the present-day, not necessarily reproducing ancient Gaelic life, or Druidic wisdom of old, because we do not know how our ancestors truly thought. However, we can speculate and interpret how we see magic within the stories, and how the seal inspires magical beliefs within us now.

The key to my own grounding was to research the past through my Welsh, Manx and Irish ancestry. It came to my awareness the purpose of any spiritual practice is to root ourselves to the land we belong to, wherever we feel is home. In rooting ourselves to the land and learning about its cultural wisdom from generations past, we ground an aspect of ourselves with newly found strength, and from there we can expand our consciousness into Otherworldly wisdoms as we embrace the Celtic mysteries in the 21$^{st}$ century. In understanding seal lore, we can discern that our ancestors had an animistic understanding that connected them to nature, not dissociate them from it. And that gave them meaning to their lives. And however far one searches for the truth of life, the journey will always circle back to our inner world. The search for magic is indeed rooted within us.

Shapeshifting is unmistakable magic, and its concept is ancient. It's an incantation we use when we wish to trick our mind and talk ourselves into being something we are not. Actors do this all the time. Indigenous shamans shapeshift by connecting to the spirit world and merge into animal form, which helps them bring back information from the Otherworld. Animals are far more advanced in their perception of spirit world than humans ever will be. They understand the unseen world, and the seals… well, they seem to know more than most. Have you ever looked into the eyes of a seal and felt transported into another realm?

The cuttlefish subtly camouflage themselves by changing colour for protection and communication. The pufferfish puff themselves up, doubling their size when the feel threatened. The complexity of cell division makes shapeshifting of humans to animals scientifically unlikely. Yet, the paranormal aspect of shapeshifting cannot be measured by science and remains a mystery. The enigma of the selchie is not a mere fayerie tale, but a belief system amongst indigenous people of the British Isles.

A belief that establishes a higher power is at play. There are tales throughout the world of humans transforming into animal form – ravens, swans, foxes, frogs, snakes, and, of course, seals. If you had the power to shapeshift, who would you be? What image does the seal awaken in your consciousness now?

# The Lore of Seals

Joseph Campbell once remarked, "Myth is the secret opening through which the inexhaustible energies of the cosmos pour into human cultural manifestation." There is a fundamental aspect for all storytellers, which is Mnemosyne – a word for the Greek Goddess of memory. Memory is a skill used in mastering storytelling and remembering timeline details. Prominent stories instil emotional touchstones for others to observe. Tales are passed down from generation to generation and are seeds of knowledge about the land, its people, and its culture. They are rich gems to hold as precious and to savour, or else die out altogether. Storytelling is about a culture's existence when there was only candlelight at night and the wind to keep one company. The lore of seals was brought to life, again and again, on cold frosty nights sat by the fireside. Storytelling for the indigenous peoples was more than just relaying a folktale.

> *Through ritual, story, and song they can transcend the ordinary limitations of time and be connected to ancestors and descendants, to those who had come before, and those still yet to come.* (Michael Newton, *A Handbook of the Scottish Gaelic World*.)

The old lore captures the heart of the Gaelic indigenous peoples. Its essence lies in travelling in your imagination to the crofts, to sit with the people in their remote abodes. In the book, *The People of the Sea* by David Thompson, Seamus Heaney describes perfectly David's ability to transport us into this world.

> *The sweetness and intimacy of David Thomson's imagination mean that he is able to bring us very close to that vanished world. His complete at-homeness in the crofts and cabins and Black Houses he entered, his ability to be all ear and eye, allow the reader to*

*access to the otherness of the minds and manner of those he met*
*there. Total respect, intuitive understanding, perfect grace and*
*perfect pitch – possessed of such gifts, he was never regarded as*
*an intruder. The naturalness of his presence seems always to have*
*made up for its unexpectedness.*

There is no word in the English language for *duthchas*, which is
a word that expresses how a culture and its people connected
to the land, and of an ancient recognition. As we grieve for
lost cultures, and embrace what is left, we get a sense of the
landscape before us, and how that seeds inspiration in our lives.
The clan culture profoundly welcomed an ancient belief around
the word *duthchas*, and today, individuals feel called to return
to their motherland and become one with it once more – where
their ancestors once belonged, and where their spirit is still
present.

There is one story I wish to share, from when I met an
elderly fisherman on Benbecula. I'd been looking out over to the
Monach Islands, when a kindly gentleman walked past me. We
passed the time of day and got chatting for a while. I asked him
if he had any seal stories to tell me. Donny revealed a wee tale of
one day when he visited Loch Eynort on the isle of South Uist.
He smiled whilst telling me of an unusual sight, explaining that
the seals were right up in the heathers; he had never seen them
so high up and so far up on land before. They were hiding far
away from the ocean as there had been sightings of orcas in the
area. The seals didn't take any chances that day. (This story was
told to me by Donny Mackay).

## Tobar an Dualchais – Seal Stories

*Tobar an Dualchais*, also known as the Kist of Riches, gives
access to sound archives in Scotland. The traditional oral stories
told in *Tobar an Dualchais* are spoken in truth. In times of old,
electricity did not exist, so there was little light to read and

storytelling was a significant pastime. Telling stories was a way to keep children occupied, especially during the winter months. Many folks couldn't read or write, so they gathered around the hearthside and made up stories, and some stories were passed on from generation to generation, and were true. As long as a stories outline is remembered, the story could be told. The tales could be short, some could last a week, and Willie Stewart once told a story called "The Wee Hen" which was ongoing for three months.

Nowadays the art of storytelling is withering, as people do not visit each other's homes any more. People stay at home, with families preferring to interact with modern day technology, or to be on their own. A sense of loneliness consumes society, and a sense of community life is ceasing to exist. Gaelic speakers become less. Storytelling dies. There are fewer storytellers today, as many have passed away. The recordings shared in *Tobar an Dualchais* are threads of knowledge which connect us to the past and speak truth about the old days.

With permission from the Scottish Archive, and the contributors and fieldworkers, I have been allowed to share some stories from the *Tobar an Dualchais*. The meaning behind the Scottish Gaelic word *dualchas* speaks of the aftereffects of the peoples being ordered to leave their homeland, and is about the heart of a people. It is a spiritual force rooting one to the land. It is blood ties. In my research for original seal lore spoken by elders who are no longer with us, I sought insight from *Tobar an Dualchais* which devotes it's time to serving the public with traditional audio recordings from the cultural heritage of Scotland's indigenous peoples.

The old stories are told in truth by people who witnessed them and passed them on to family and friends in the villages where they lived. It is okay to write about the traditional folklore, and seal lore and to share these stories with wider communities. But all the while we must remember to be precise in acknowledging where the stories originated from, to respect and pay tribute to the original storyteller. By retelling the old stories as accurately as possible with a sense of logic and rationality; seeing the lessons within a tale, and allowing inspiration to wash over us as we contemplate what this lore means to us now; we need to remember that the old stories are multi-faceted and can take a lifetime to learn.

The initial story I wish to share from *Tobar an Dulchais* is about the seal skin tobacco pouch which seemed to have magical powers. This story is spoken in Scottish Gaelic by Archie MacAulay. Archie spoke about having a seal skin tobacco pouch or *spliuchan* in Scottish Gaelic, tying together a ball of wool, and a small piece of sealskin, and putting them in a trouser or coat pocket. As the sealskin and wool sat next to each other, when the tide was coming in land at hight tide, the wool was meant to wind around the sealskin, and when the surge of sea was flowing outwards at low tide, the wool would unwind. Archie knew of a man who tried this out and said it was a fact. (The seal skin tobacco pouch, Contributor's name: Archie MacAulay, Fieldworker's name: Donald Archie MacDonald (SA ref: 1963.007) School of Scottish Studies Archives. University of Edinburgh.)

In the olden days, seafaring men revered the seal as good luck and liked to keep their flippers – sometimes to eat them. But it was the seal's right flipper that had special magical qualities when made into a purse. It was believed the changing colour of the purse would foretell the condition of the ocean tides.

Seal hunting is a controversial topic. In the United Kingdom it is an offence to take, injure or deliberately or carelessly kill a seal under the Conservation of Seals Act 1970. There are exceptions, and one who is disabled or hurt can be caught for rehabilitation purposes, but must then be released back into the wild when it is well, or housed at a sanctuary if there is no chance of recovery. In bygone days, pinnipeds were hunted in

Celtic waters, especially at the rock of Haskeir situated eight miles away from North Uist, where an annual seal hunt took place. The only people who did not take part in this hunt were the Clan MacCodrum. Oak clubs were used to kill the them, and quite often seal oil was used for medicinal purpose. The only side-effect was the dreadful smell from the oil. Here is a story of how seal oil was used in Shetland.

*When Brucie Henderson was a boy, sheep were dipped in seal oil, which was bought in barrels and boiled with Stockholm tar until it formed a dark syrup-like mixture. The sheep were dipped by hand. A girl would open the sheep's fleece along the rig (spine) and the dip was poured on from a can with a stroop (spout) and worked into the fleece. This was continued in strips down the belly. The seal oil made the sheep grow terrible (huge) fleeces of wool. The sun and weather purified the wool when dipping and clipping (shearing).* (Sheep Dipping in Shetland with Seal Oil and Stockholm Tar, Contributor's name: Brucie Henderson, Fieldworker's name: Alan Bruford (SA ref: 1970.241) School of Scottish Studies Archives. University of Edinburgh.)

Just to the north of North Uist lies the Isle of Berneray. It is a place filled with Gaelic history, and where many seals gather in a bob on the harbour bay area, and can be observed at a safe distance from seal viewing point. Catherine Dix lived on Berneray. Catherine was born in 1890 and was a Gaelic bard known for her exceptional talent in recalling hundreds of songs, stories, and poems. Catherine gave an understanding of the Gaelic-speaking community in the middle of the 20th century. Catherine's home was a traditional thatched cottage, positioned beside the ocean. Today in that place, only a ruin remains.

In earlier times the character of 'filidh' or professional clan bard was held in high regard by Gaelic society. After the clan systems broke down, the Gaelic traditions continued in villages on the Scottish islands, and the bards were known as bàird baile or poets of the village.

Vashti Bunyan, who lived on the island in the late 1960s, said of her: "She was the kindest of women, the fiercest of souls, and I adored her."

In *Tobar an Dualchais* Catherine shares a song about seal lore. It is a *pìobaireachd* – "an act of playing the bagpipes".

*The contributor says that this song was heard coming out of the chimney when lots of seals were killed. In the song the seal laments having been killed and it is given a human personality. The contributor says that her father used to play the tune on the chanter.* (Spòg Mo Ròin Gun D' Fhuair Mi, Contributor's name: Catherine Dix Fieldworker's name: Ian Paterson (SA ref: 1969.083) School of Scottish Studies Archives. University of Edinburgh.)

There are many tales told throughout history of bad luck befalling people who hurt seals. Here is a true account. Brucie Henderson recounts a tale:

*A sick seal came ashore in Mid Yell Voe and crawled into a field where he ate lubba (rough grass). A hunter shot and skinned the animal. Shortly after, the hunter went to shoot seals in the precipice of the banks (cliffs), and a stone rolled down and broke his leg. He lay on a ledge till he was rescued by two boys. He lay in a stranger's house for six weeks until his leg mended. The hunter went on to live till a ripe old age, but he never shot seals again.* (A hunter suffers after killing a sick seal, Contributor's name: Brucie Henderson, Fieldworker's name: Iain Calum Maclean (SA ref: 1955.097) School of Scottish Studies Archives. University of Edinburgh.)

I believe we have the ability to connect with spirit world, to perceive the subtle spiritual nature of the land and its creatures, and to hear animals speak in the form of *animal communication*. Here is a true account of when Mac Ruairidh heard a spirit voice from the Otherworld.

*Mac Ruairidh left early in the morning to hunt seals. He fell asleep in his hiding place. Three times he heard a warning voice. He took off with fright. Fire hit the place where he had been sitting. The contributor heard this story from his Uncle Neil.* (A warning voice, Contributor's name: James Robertson. Fieldworker's name: Donald Archie MacDonald (SA ref: 1963.007) School of Scottish Studies Archives. University of Edinburgh.)

George Peterson shared his story about the seals:

*A crew of men went to the Ve Skerries off Papa Stour to hunt for seals. The belief at this time was that some seals could change into humans and come ashore, by taking off their skins. The men landed on the skerries and started clubbing seals. The weather deteriorated and they had to run for the boat. One man got left behind and the others couldn't get near enough to pick him up.*

*The man was looking for a skrivvik (cleft in the rocks) where he could shelter, when he heard a voice. It was a giant mother seal lurking in the scruff (surface) of the shoormal (edge of the water). The seal offered to take him to Papa if he would fetch the skin of a young seal that was hanging up in a skeo (stone beach hut) at Culla Voe and lay it below the flod (hight tide) mark. He promised, and got on the seal's back, after having cut slots in her skin to hang onto. When he got ashore, he fetched the hide and put it in the ebb. As he left, he saw two seals swimming away from the shore. He went home and was sitting having a cup of tea when the door opened and in came the three men who had left him on the Ve Skerries.* (A seal hunter was saved by a giant seal in exchange for its pup's life, Contributor's name: George Peterson, Fieldworker's name: Alan Bruford (SA ref: 1974.204) School of Scottish Studies Archives. University of Edinburgh.)

The seal people were also known as the Finn folk of Norway. The human-like qualities of pinnipeds are highlighted in the story of a seal-man wounded by a fisherman, where later he returned the fisherman's knife. Seals have human-like characteristics: they are attracted to music; the pups make the sounds similar to human babies, the adults' sounds are like drowning men; and they shed tears.

*A Shetland man hunting seals knifed one on the seashore. It escaped into the sea (with the knife sticking in it). Sometime afterwards, the man was in Norway. He went into a house where an old man was sitting at the fire looking at him closely. The old man reached up and pulled a knife from somewhere and asked if the Shetland man had seen it before. The hunter knew this was the seal he'd stabbed. Robert Bairnson heard the story a long time ago. He comments that there is much more detail than he can recall. (A Shetland seal hunter encountered a man whom he'd wounded in the form of a seal, Contributor's name: Robert Bairnson, Fieldworker's name: Prof. Tadaaki Miyake (SA ref: 1972.240) School of Scottish Studies Archives. University of Edinburgh.)*

I hope you have enjoyed these tales from *Tobar an Dualchais*, which is a treasure trove of wisdom and truth. Do you have any seal stories to share?

# Celtic Seal-Folk Tales

Seals spend eighty percent of their lives in the ocean; their heart is the ocean where they are self-confident and where they freely roam. The seal people are a reality and core belief among travellers, crofters, and fishermen in the northern regions, on the west coast Islands of Scotland, Orkney, and Shetland. Seal lore invokes an adoration for all living creatures.

Selchie legends go further afield, to Greenland, Northern Canada, and Alaska, where the Inuit people there are called *the People of the Seal*. In Iceland, the Faroe Islands and Norway; where there were the Sea Sami peoples. Selchie stories travelled throughout the north and east with the Vikings, and are more isolated stories rather than the deeply held beliefs of the people in Scotland, and Orkney.

The tales of old were kept as sacred information and were rarely shared. Information was guarded, to be kept within family units or local communities. It is only through the impressive works of Duncan Williamson, David Thompson, and John MacAulay that we get to hear about the seal people. It's crucial to keep these stories as sacred, and share them with the greatest of integrity through understanding we are not only hearing seal lore, but we are feeling into our ancestors' triumphs, and tears.

The story of *Black Angus, the Seal-Man and St Columba* tells the tale of Black Angus, a selchie from North Uist who had a conflict of interests over whose spiritual faith was right or wrong, with St Columba on Iona. St Columba painted Black Angus as evil and of no good. Black Angus was said to have placed a curse on St Columba. But did he really? From the book, *The Isle of Dreams* by Fiona Macleod written in 1913 (page 48),

*The holy man had wandered on to where the rocks are, opposite the Soa. Of a sudden he came upon a great black seal, lying silent on the rocks, with wicked eyes. 'My blessings upon you, O Ron,' he said, with the good kind courteousness that was his. 'Droch spadadh ort,' answered the seal, 'a bad end to you Colum of the Gown.' 'Sure now,' said Colum angrily, 'I am knowing by that curse that you are no friend of Christ, but of the evil pagan faith out of the north. For here I am known ever as Colum the White, or as Colum the Saint; and it is only the Picts and wanton Normen who deride me because of the holy white robe I wear.' 'Well, well,' replied the seal, speaking the good Gaelic as though it were the tongue of the deep sea, as God knows it may be for you, I, or the blind wind can say; 'Well, well, let that thing be: it's a wave-way here or a wave-way there. But now if it is a Druid you are, whether of fire, or of Christ, be telling me where my woman is, and where my little daughter.'*

The story goes on to say:

*At this, Colum looked at him for a long while. Then he knew. 'It is a man you were once, O Ron? And with that thick Gaelic that you have, it will be out of the north isles that you come?' 'That is a true thing.' 'Now I am for knowing at last who and what you are. You are one of the race of Odrum the Pagan?' 'Well, I am not denying it, Colum. And what is more, I am Angus MacOdrum, Aonghas mac Torcall Mhic Odrum, and the name I am known by is Black Angus.' 'A fitting name too,' said Colum the Holy, 'because of the black sin in your heart, and the black end God has in store for you.' At that Black Angus laughed. 'Why is there laughter upon you, Man-Seal?' 'Well, it is because of the good company I'll be having.'*

Magic and Christianity did not mix well, yet a few Christian ministers supported Gaelic cultural traditions and belief systems. There were few early Christian versions of seal lore that were told in pure light, as they were often spoken of in contempt in an attempt to purge indigenous Gaelic beliefs. A few Christian ambassadors respected the pre-Christian stories, songs, and beliefs of the Gaels, and you will find such honouring in the writings of Reverend John Gregorson Campbell, who was a Free Church Minister for Tiree and Coll parishes in Argyll. In the Introduction to the book, *Clan Traditions and Popular Tales of the Western Highlands and Islands* by John Campbell Gregorson, Alfred Nutt states:

> *We do not go far wrong in conjecturing that the minister's zealous interest for the preservation and elucidation of the native traditions was not the least potent of his claims upon the respect and love of his flock. How keenly the Highlander still treasures these faint echoes of the past glories and sorrows of his race is known to all who have won his confidence.*

Seal lore invokes an awakening of the soul. The old Gaelic tales inspire faith, unity of spirit, and most of all love. Duncan Williamson shared:

> *But I learned most of the seal stories I know directly from working with crofters, and fishermen along Loch Fyne. These people didn't frankly tell stories to just anybody. They had very guarded attitudes towards their knowledge. It was sacred information told to them by their family and they meant to keep it in their family. It was only by me partly coaxing them and by accident and my being interested that I ever opened them up to get one seal story from them! Now the important thing to remember is that these stories were never made; they were never set to any pattern. They were just something strange according to them that actually took place. It was family history; that's the truth.* (Duncan Williamson, *Land of the Seal People*).

Stories are the roots, the bones, the life blood of a people; the travellers did not go to school, so the stories were their education. Folk tales are instruments of truth, as they talk about the sacredness of life. The old cultural tales contain our ancestor's wisdoms, and the *genius loci* that resides in the wilderness. What legends dwell on your land of birth? Seek them, and you will better understand your history, and yourself. Edward Burnett Taylor explains:

*The poet contemplates the same natural world as the man of science, but in his so different craft strives to render difficult thought easy by making it visible and tangible, above all by referring the being and movement of the world to such personal life as his hearers feel within themselves, and thus working out in far stretched fancy the maxim that 'Man is the measure of all things'. Let but the key be recovered to this mythic dialect.*

The bards of our culture, old and new, keep the magic of storytelling alive. For if these repositories were to be lost, we would lose an essential part of our own remembering.

*The myths shaped out of those endless analogies between man and nature are the soul of all poetry, onto those half-human stories still so full to us of unfading life and beauty, are the masterpieces of an art belonging rather to the past than the present. The growth of myth has been checked by science, it is dying of weights and measures, of proportions and specimens – it's not only dying, but also half dead, and students are anatomising it. In this world one must do what one can, and if the moderns cannot feel myth as their forefathers did, at least they can analyse it. There is a kind of intellectual frontier with in which he must be who will investigate it, and it is our fortune that we live near this frontier-line and can go in and out.* (Edward Burnett Tylor, *Primitive Culture*, published in 1871).

And so, the myths and legends of ancient cultures are a rich tapestry of tales. The old seal stories share humanities carelessness inflicted on nature; a neglect which is often caused through lack of understanding, and they teach us to walk humbly alongside nature, treating her with more kindness, just as we would our own friends, family, and mother.

## Master Storyteller of Selchie Folklore, Duncan Williamson

The late Duncan Williamson, master storyteller, influenced my heart and thoughts around seal lore. His spirit flows through the written books and has been influential in guiding me to look beyond, into the divine spark of nature and the seal. I contacted Linda Williamson about sharing one of Duncan's stories, explaining my wish to write this book. And I shared the story of me saving the three-day old seal pup at Boscastle, and of my love of pinnipeds. To love a wild animal is something I can't quite put into words. Wild animals are meant to stay wild; it would be unhealthy for seals to become accustomed to being near humans by making them reliant upon us for food, as this would not help them to be self-sufficient. It's crucial to give seals the space they need to be wild and free, and love them safely from a *distance*. My seal mother's heart knows this.

In my enquiring conversations about Duncan's life as a storyteller and member of the traveller community in Scotland, Linda shared:

*Yes, the tinkers or Travelling People as they are officially known, a recognised Ethnic Minority (2011 census), are an indigenous people of the UK, Scotland, and Ireland. The Travellers have been in Scotland from the Palaeolithic era. They are not gypsies. They are not cultivators and farmers. They have always been hunter-gatherers, tribal and racially distinct. Duncan's family were descended from Orcadian bull breeders. There is a large Norse element in his ancestry.*

Reading *Tales of the Seal People* by Duncan Williamson touched my spirit in a way stories never had before. In particular, Duncan's story of 'The Silkie Painter' resonated with the story of when I found Elizabeth, the wild Atlantic grey seal pup. The character, Mary, although living in a different situation, reminded me of myself, and how I took it upon myself to rescue the little seal pup that fateful night at Boscastle – a story which I will share at the end of the book. The seal illuminates us with rich lessons: be kind to them, and they will treat you well; do harm to any of them, and they will teach you a lesson. The stories of old show children and adults right from wrong, and they touch your heart and soul if you let them. Duncan Williamson spoke a truth about a universal law, and of how important it is to protect and care for nature and the wild animals, to protect the stone people, the plant people, our animal family, as we are all related and interdependent on some level. Duncan explained:

*Seal folk are supposed to help you, do good things for you. They've never been known to do anyone any evil! So, the story I'm going to tell you is about an old woman and a seal. It was told to me many, many years ago by a man who believed this happened. His name was Niall MacCallum, the old stonemason I was apprenticed to when I was fifteen at Auchindrain. It was a story kept in his family and in ours. The Highlanders were a close-knitted kind of folk and did not go telling the whole world about their stories and tales and cracks because people would have thought they were crazy. But Neil maintained that his great-great-granny told him this one because she had the picture in her house...* (Tales of the Seal People by Duncan Williamson, 'The Silkie Painter'.)

Duncan's story, 'The Silkie Painter', is one which I retell in the passages below, and which Linda Williamson gave me permission to do so.

In a quaint little cottage on the west coast of Scotland lived an old fisherman and his wife called Mary and John. They both lived a simple life. Mary kept hens and goats and used to take the eggs, and goats' milk to the village, where everybody knew everyone, and John caught fish for a living. They lived a peaceful life, and had no rifts with anyone, apart from the fact that John hated seals. He disliked them with a vengeance because they were always getting in his fishing nets, ripping them up, and eating his catch. He was always moaning about them to Mary, but Mary being a kindly lady would say, 'John, the seals have as much right to be here as the rest of us.' When Mary had any spare time, she would walk down to the beach front and collect dulse seaweed. After stringing the dulse out to dry, and a man would come and buy it from her to make perfume out of it and wot not.

One day Mary was collecting dulse when she happened upon a baby seal on the shoreline, after checking to see if its mother was nearby and after she could not see it anywhere Mary removed her apron and placed the seal in it for easy transportation. When Mary arrived back home with the wee pup John was aghast to see it, and said he would not have it in the house. But Mary felt sorry for the helpless pup and wanted to care for it, so she ignored John, and placed it in a basket by the fire and gathered some milk to feed it. John complained incessantly about the seals, they seemed to fuel his anger and bitterness. But Mary loved the little seal as if it were her own, and the pup loved Mary and followed her everywhere.

A few days after the pup's rescue took place there was a knock at the door, Mary went to see who it was and standing there was a fine-looking young man who was looking for a room for a couple of weeks. He introduced himself as Iain, and said he was an artist. Mary and John did have a room spare and welcomed him inside their property. Iain settled in quickly, it felt like home to him, and Mary and John loved him being there. Iain joined the couple for evening meals, and they became fond of each other quickly, but the strange thing was Iain never took any notice of the seal pup who rested in the basket by the fire. I mean, it's odd to have a seal indoors, but he never said anything. Iain felt familiar to Mary, she had an innate feeling she knew him, but couldn't put her finger on where she had met him before. The two men hit it off so well and John asked Iain if he would like to help him one day with his fishing nets. John wished he had a son like Iain, and Iain was more than happy to help the old man with anything he could.

To cut a long story short one morning they both went fishing, but whilst out at sea, darkness descended in the sky as a storm was brewing, the boat was a good mile away from the shore and the nets were still out. The gales blew and it was so fierce they could barely make it back to shore. Both Iain and John took an oar and rowed as fast as they could, but the waves became high and furious, and the boat overturned. The sea swallowed Iain up. John cried out, 'Iain, Iain take the oar,' but Iain was nowhere to be seen. John continued to swim to the mainland which was a way in the distance, but it was further than he thought. He became exhausted and overcome with sadness as he realised, he would never make it. The oar fell from his hands and John sank beneath the turbulent water when he felt an object underneath him. John thought it was a giant log, when it occurred to him it was a large grey seal. Both shocked, and relieved John clung to the seal for dear life, and it swam swiftly, and took John safely to the shore. The seal left John lying on the beach, then turned and swam off into the raging sea.

Mary had been pacing the shoreline, looking to see where Iain and her husband were. The rain lashed down, and she was so relieved to see John lying on the beach. She ran over and pulled him up. John was in a dreadful state. 'Iain has gone Mary; we have lost him. The storm capsized the boat, and he didn't make it, we will never see him again.'

Both of them slowly walked home, and when inside Mary settled John by the warmth of the fire, and wrapped him in a thick woollen blanket, right next to the seal pup. 'Mary, a seal came and saved my life, he saved me, bought me to shore,' he kept repeating this to himself. 'And after everything I have said about the seals, one came and saved my life.' John vowed from that moment on he would never say anything unpleasant about the seals again.

Morning came, and John and Mary were still in shock from the previous day's happenings. The storm had passed, and the weather was again fair, and the ocean was tranquil. At midday they both took a walk to the village to report Iain as missing, but the strange thing was that no one had ever seen or heard of Iain, they had no idea who they were talking about. No one knew him. Later, the police constable turned up at their home and they told him the story of Iain the artist who came to stay for a few weeks, and how fast he became a great friend to the both of them and the terrible storm that overturned John's fishing boat, and how the water swallowed Iain up. But they never mentioned the seal who saved John's life.

They took the policeman upstairs to the room where Iain had been staying to see if he had any paperwork, but there were no personal items. The bed hadn't been slept in or touched. Iain left nothing apart from a painting which faced outwards at the window. A canvas picture. John walked over to the window and turned the painting around and exclaimed, 'Mary, you would not believe it.' The picture was of an old woman collecting dulse on the beach, and there was a baby seal, the exact image of Mary and the seal pup. The old woman kept silent. John asked Mary, 'How did Iain manage to paint such a perfect picture of you both?' 'Oh, I probably told him how I found the pup, and he painted it from memory.' The policeman let them both know there was little he could do about the situation now, and of how it was a tragedy. Time passed by, and there never was another word about Iain, he was never seen again. A while later the seal pup had reached a considerable weight and was fit enough to fend for itself, so it came time for it to be released back into the sea. John and Mary carried it down to the shoreline and watched as the seal hobbled into the ocean. The old man never complained about seals again and whenever the woman went down to the beachfront to collect dulse seaweed and saw the seals floating nearby, she would look over at them and smile. 'Oh Iain,' she said, 'you certainly made your point.' She knew Iain was a selchie of the sea.

Duncan's stories portray concepts that are beyond our understanding. Seal stories have a certain degree of ambiguity which we can observe with a sense of wonder in our heart. The tales of the selchie ask us to walk in faith, as selchies are from a spiritual realm. They behold a sacred truth that belongs to the great mystery itself. We must endeavour to share kindness with all we meet. Kindness is key to our happiness, for we cannot live without others by our side; it would be impossible. The old stories teach us to forge admirable relationships with humans, animals, plants, and stone people, and in turn good will come back to us. I believe, out of all Duncan's stories, this was one of the most potent messages he conveyed.

# The Selchie Maiden

Betwixt land and deep-blue sea, light and the unlit, love and lamenting; the song of the seals leads us home to that comfortable space of peace, home, to our true natures once more. The story of the selchie maiden left me feeling melancholic. Her yearning for the ocean whilst trapped on land without her seal skin was tragic. I understood the selchie maiden had had her freedom and silver-grey skin stolen; trapped upon land, her soul was left feeling incomplete. Eventually she finds freedom, but at the detriment of having to leave her children behind, as she returns to dwell in the depths of the ocean as her seal self – her real self.

The selchie maiden story is relatable to many men and women around the world. Within the contemporary selchie poem *'Maighdean-ròin'*, performed by Marcas Mac an Tuairneir in the film/poem of the same name, in Scottish Gaelic, Marcas weaves powerful words of the journey encountered by women or men who have had their inner power stolen. Culminating in the Selchie's eventual regaining ultimate freedom and renewal, Marcas of the poem remarks,

> *The selkie story is a metaphor for intimate partner violence, something which impacts women throughout the world. In the poem, the selkie looks to the day that never comes, hoping to escape from her partner, encouraged by the yellow sands of the beach and remembering back to her 'yellow' halcyon days.*

Halcyon days are referred to as *'làithean buidhe'* (yellow days) in the Gaelic language. For those stuck in disrespectful relationships or healing from past trauma, for those who feel generally trapped, the selchie maiden may strike a chord with you. The seal metaphorically teaches us about finding freedom and our true selves on a deeper soul level, of reclamation after trauma and assault. And this reclamation can happen time and time again. As humans, we may need to adjust our own seal skins and wear freedom powerfully, honouring it, and never letting that freedom go, whatever the cost. I suppose you could say I found my own spiritual seal skin and will never abandon it again. My promise to the spirit of the seal is to honour freedom, and if someone is not filled with patience and kindness, then I will let them go. The wisest advice I was given was to "keep the gentle folk near," and life has wielded tenderness since. The magic of the seal reminds us of our innate power to honour ourselves, and see through anything that takes our power away.

I want to share one of the most widespread selchie stories. The selchie maiden is told throughout many continents and has unique threads in each story line. On Orkney, the seal partner is a male selchie, and on other continents the selchie is female. Stories about the selchie maiden left a sadness within me as I navigated the depth of injustice in its meaning. Although seemingly filled with romantic love and a simple family life, the true meaning could be interpreted as a life filled with unkindness, manipulation, and the stripping away of human rights which many people can identify with. This is why the story is relevant today. The selchie, though, always regains its freedom.

I hope you are sitting comfortably, gathered round a fire, hot drink at the ready, as I share one of the famous selchie stories about Roderic MacCodrum, known as a MacCodrum of the seals. Roderic, who was a fisherman, lived on the Isle of Berneray on the peaceful Outer Hebrides of Scotland. It is one of the oldest geological islands in the world, where the Lewisian gneiss sings its wisdom into our bones; a place where the land, and the Otherworld, exist only three feet apart.

Roderic MacCodrum from the Clan Donald, a family of the Clan MacDonald, lived alone, and it often crossed his mind about finding a wife, but he never quite found someone who lit his fire. One day, Roderic took to the beach where his fishing boat lay. It was a fine day, the sun gleamed through cloud-filled skies, and it was a mighty fine calm ocean, like a mill pond. He was just about to untie his boat when he heard a melodious voice coming from over the rocks. He walked quietly over to take a closer look, as if eclipsed by the heavenly voices. Angelic light filled the air, and as he peered over the rocks, there were three maidens dancing, their milky pure skins glistening like moonshine, their hair long, dark as the night sky. Roderic could not believe his eyes. He stayed there for a time, which seemed to last forever. Aware he did not wish to startle them, he made his way back over the rocks, taking it steady not to slip on the seaweed that had gathered from the recent heavy storms. As he walked away, he noticed three silvery, silky skins left on the sand; they were the most beautiful pelts he had ever seen. The silver-grey fur had golden streaks and dark, jet back blotches, but oh so very beautiful and the softest fur he had ever touched.

Now, Roderic had never stolen anything in his whole life, but this temptation was too much to bear, and he took one of the silky skins home and buried it. It was his treasure, like Gollum's golden ring. Not one thought crossed his mind that it was not his to keep. Later that evening, as he was eating his hearty tattie drottle by the warmth of the log fire, he heard a knock at the door. There, standing naked, with skin the colour of the moon and hair as black as the night sky, a maiden stood before him. "I have lost my skin, please could you help me find it," she cried. Roderic took the maiden in and placed a blanket around her shoulders, all the while reassuring her that he would help her look for it.

Days and nights passed by, and the maiden stayed at Roderic's home. He read her stories and she cooked for him; she was patient, graceful, kind-natured, and peace emanated from her. Quietness eclipsed her as if she was always listening to the sea, hearing the calls of the seals, of the ocean's song that

Roderic could not find in himself. He fell desperately in love with her, and one day on a waning moon they married. Roderic never mentioned the silky skin, as truth be told, he had fallen in love with the maiden and did not want to let her go. In his selfishness, he kept the secret of her hidden skin. Time passed by and they had two children – a beautiful girl with deep brown eyes and hair as black as the night sky; and the boy, too, had the deepest brown eyes with chestnut hair. Roderic had blue grey eyes, so they resembled their mother's genes.

Over time the selchie maiden became melancholic. She lived in a charming cottage by the ocean, and would often gaze out into the horizon and think of her true home – home beneath the ocean's waves, amidst the vermillion-coloured seaweed, with her family the seals. Her heart ached to go home, her skin became as grey as a thick mist, and her hair dry and brittle, she looked like a walking ghost. She carried on her married life with Roderic and her children, and she was a good wife and no-one could have been a better, caring mother. The village would comment that she always had a far-off look in her eyes, as if she was in another world, and they often found it difficult to communicate with her, calling her strange. Time passed and her children grew. One day, Roderic went out fishing early one morning and the children were playing in the bedrooms. The selchie maiden was hanging the washing out, but the wind was picking up, and she would not have long before the rains came down. Her son came running out of the house. "Mamma, look what I have found in your bedroom under the floorboard. It is a blanket made of pure silky fur." The maiden gasped and ran towards her pelt. It had been right under her feet all the while. Every night she fell asleep, she had been sleeping on her freedom, for the pelt was hidden right under a loose floorboard in her bedroom.

She held her children close to her and knew she had to act fast to escape to her freedom before her husband returned home later that evening. With her children's heads close to her belly, she embraced them and said, "Mamma has to leave, but you will always find me if you look out to the ocean. Sing and I will hear you." The children didn't quite understand, but a part of them knew she was a selchie, and she had always told them stories about the seals and the kings and queens of the sea. Of a royal palace in Norway, where three princesses were put under the spell of a wicked witch as she turned them into seals, and of how they had found home on the tranquil and holy isles of the Outer Hebrides, where they felt safe and free from harm. The children eventually realised that their mother was talking about her own story. They watched her clad herself in the precious silver-grey seal skin, and they held each other's hand tightly. "You have my blood, dear children; therefore you, too, are a part of the ocean and the seal people; you, too, are the selchie bloodlines. I love you with all of my heart, and I will think of you every day. But I have to go now. I must return home."

Tears streamed down their faces, and the mother's heart was torn into pieces. With those last words, she turned and went into the sea, where two other seals were waiting for her. They leapt out of the ocean with joy and cried out – a haunting cry that chills one to the bone.

The husband came home from fishing and found the children entwined in a sorrowful hug. "She's gone, Father. She has gone." He fell to his knees and prayed to God for all of his mistakes and lies, and he was never quite the same as grief gripped his heart for the rest of his days, and he and his children became known as the MacCodrum of the seals. And in the coming years, when Roderic and his son went fishing, they took care never to harm a seal. Often, the children would stand on golden sand and look out into the white horses' waves and see their mother pop her head out of the waters. She never did leave the Isle of Berneray shores.

This story is told throughout Scotland in different versions. On the Isle of Berneray, the selchie maiden is one of the Norwegian King's daughters, and her pelt was buried rather than placed in a chest; other continents state the seal pelts were hidden in chests with keys, such as in the Faeroe Isles; and there is a story from Deerness on mainland Orkney, where a sea-kist (chest) is used.

*The young man had locked her selkie skin away in a big kist, and hid the key. She said that this was for the best, as she had put her seal days behind her. They lived together in happiness for years and had bonnie bairns together.* (Tom Muir, author of 'The Selkie Wife' *The Mermaid Bride and other Orkney folk tales*.)

In Iceland, a man from Myrdalur marries a selchie and uses a key to hide her skin. Finding the key to the chest where the selchie skin is hidden is metaphorically finding the key to your own soul. The symbol of a key inspired the front cover of this book. The seal dives deep into Staffa Cave near Iona in the Inner Hebrides of Scotland and notices an ornate silver key – the key to freedom. The cover was designed by Leanne Daphne, a professional illustrator who lives in Scotland. Unfortunately, the selchie maiden stories never rejoice in a happily ever after, as she usually returns to the ocean. One cannot trap a selchie woman or keep her prisoner, for she will *always* find a way to freedom.

In Celtic mythology, the animal kingdom are our teachers. As we sense the world of the seal, we begin to feel closer to all aspects of the ocean, and humanity. The seal's symbology represents an individual energy. We can indeed imagine a metaphorical seal skin wrapped around us, a pelt as soft as silk, and where the sensitivity of the seal becomes us.

For a moment, let's look at the selchie, of ways in which we have lost or had our own seal skin stolen. We can lose power throughout our lives, and not realise until we become withdrawn and feel helpless. Metaphorically reclaiming our seal skins requires us to investigate forgotten parts of ourselves, where we have given up on hope, and faith, and lost aspects of our freedom. By reclaiming the wild wisdom of our innate natures, the wise woman, the wise man. Take a moment to reflect. Which aspect of your inner power has been stolen? Who or what stole this inner power from your wild selves? How do you think you will reclaim your sense of self and re-ignite your creative fire and imagination?

## Meditation to reclaim your seal skin

*Firstly, ground yourself by imagining yourself connected to the landscape around you.*

*Close your eyes and gently relax.*

*Take some deep breaths and let go of all your thoughts from the day.*

*Feel the power of your breath move through you, then bring your mind into the present moment.*

*Continue to breathe deeply and feel your body go deeper, and deeper, into a state of peace.*

*Imagine you are sitting in a large, secluded cave, situated by the beach; there is a fire in the centre that lights up the cave's walls and warms your soul. You sit half-naked by the heat of the flames. Many seals hobble up from the beach and gather around the fire to join you. They lift their heads in joy, eyes sparkling with compassion, acknowledging your presence, chanting, barking, grunting, and roaring a homecoming song – your homecoming song.*

*Beside you lies a beautiful silver-grey seal pelt. You reach down to pull the pelt close, and as you tenderly hold it in your arms you give thanks for the seals' wisdoms.*

*Rest for a while and let your thoughts wander. Ask yourself if there are times when you have had your power stripped away.*

*Acknowledge the people who stole your inner power and say to yourself, "I take back my power, and reclaim my sense of self. I no* longer allow anyone to steal my time or energy without my permission. I create boundaries for my health and wellbeing. I am not afraid to say no."

See your vital life force returning to you. A rose-pink energy fills your heart, and you feel yourself return to a state of peace.

See parts of your soul returning

You place the seal skin on your shoulders, as a talisman. It protects you.

The seal pelt sets boundaries. It teaches you to listen to your intuition and when it's necessary to say no. Or when to walk away from a situation that is disempowering you.

The seal skin becomes a part of your soul. It represents your wild nature, your wholeness and freedom, reminding you of the beauty and the peace that is inside of you. So, create what you love, and do not wait for time to pass you by. Allow the spirit of Awen to re-ignite the free-flowing spirit of inspiration, imagination, awe, and wonder within you.

If you feel inclined, you may wish to forgive those who stole your power, but there is no need to do this – only if you feel it is right to do so.

Gently bring yourself out of the meditation and ground yourself.

Taking a meditation journey to remember your sense of self, and soul's freedom may take time. But you can return to this cave where the seals sing, and remember your unique selchie song of reclamation and homecoming whenever you wish to.

# Seal Lore of the Faeroe Isles, Orkney, Wales, and Ireland

If you ever dream about crossing paths with a male selchie, take a walk on the coastline and release seven tears into the ocean. Legend says a male selchie will appear, bringing intense, and overwhelming love to unhappy lives. They seek out forlorn, and isolated women, normally wives whose husbands are out at sea for days on end. However, they can only stay for a short time before returning to the ocean deep, leaving her heartbroken. They possess long dark hair, fair skin, and have been known to treacherously sink ships that hunt seals.

## Faeroe Seal Lore

Occasionally, seals incite revenge on those who hurt them, yet if you are kind, you will be granted a good life. There is a story about a vengeful selkie who lived on the Faeroe Islands, and was called *Kopakonan*, which is Faroese for the seal woman. In Mikladalur – on the island of Kalsoy – where this story is from, a statue of the seal woman was elegantly crafted and placed on a rock by the ocean in honour or perhaps to appease the hurt spirit of the seal woman. It was thought she placed a curse over the village through seeking revenge after her husband and son had been murdered by a fisherman. Many tales have taken place since this curse, where men go mad or lose their lives; all because of the vengeful selchie curse. The seal is believed to be a forgiving soul, but in this instance on the island of Kalsoy, she was filled with retribution.

Folklore stories are profound. Narratives explore transformation, re-connecting to the self, kindness, compassion, justice, love, and loss. The selchie stories are sorrowful and evoke remembering's of our own loss and grief, and is the reason why we are so moved by them.

## Orkney Seal Lore

One of Orkney's most haunting ballads is about a male selchie who lived on a rocky islet too small for human inhabitation, but perfect for the seals to rest their weary heads. It is known as Sule Skerry, a part of Stromness parish in Orkney, which lies thirty-two nautical miles west of Orkney Mainland, and is not to be mixed-up with Sula Sgeir. In the ballad, a fair maiden from Orkney falls in love with a selchie. Now, from what I have heard, this wouldn't be difficult, because they are incredibly beautiful, charismatic, and pure of spirit. The fair maiden from Orkney and the selchie had a son together, but soon after, he disappears from their lives.

In later years, having brought the son up on her own, the fair maiden from Orkney happens to cross paths with a large grey seal on the shoreline. The seal whispers a truth to her, "I am a man upon the land, and I am a silkie in the sea, and when I'm far and far from land, my home it is in Sule Skerry." It dawns on the kindly woman that the grey seal is none other than her selchie lover – a fayerie changeling whom she had met many moons ago. As is the nature of selchies, always on the move, mysterious, and aloof, he vanishes, and she doesn't cross paths with him again for seven years – seven being a magical number within Celtic tradition, and which represents courage, protection, and enchantment.

After seven years the grey seal returns and gifts his son a golden chain, which shimmered golden like the sun. The boy leaves his mother and travels with his father to sea, leaving her in deep grief. Eventually, she marries again and happiness reigns once more. But fate has a funny way of shifting reality, and one day her new husband goes out hunting, and shoots two grey seals – one large grey seal and the other a younger one. Around the neck of the young seal hung a sunlit golden chain, which the hunter takes home to his new wife. Upon receiving the gift, she breaks down in tears with the revelation that her son no longer lives.

This ballad originated in the Orkney Islands. Francis J. Child & Child Ballads: 113. "The English and Scottish Popular Ballads" 1882–1898, and is an authoritative collection of folk ballads.

Version one is where the lovers – the seal man and human – meet:

*The silkie be a creature strange,*
*He rises from the sea to change,*
*Into a man, a weird one he,*
*When home it is in Skule Skerrie.*

*When he be man, he takes a wife,*
*When he be beast, he takes her life.*
*Ladies, beware of him who be –*
*A silkie come from Skule Skerrie.*

*His love they willingly accept,*
*But after they have loved and slept,*
*Who is the monster that they see?*
*'Tis "Silkie" come from Skule Skerrie.*

*A maiden from the Orkney Isles,*
*A target for his charm, his smiles,*
*Eager for love, no fool was she,*
*She knew the secret of Skule Skerrie.*

*And so, while Silkie kissed the lass,*
*She rubbed his neck with Orkney grass,*

*This had the magic power, you see —*
*To slay the beast from Skule Skerrie.*

This ballad is Child Ballad number thirteen.
Version two is where the seal father and son are murdered:

*An earthly nourris sits and sings,*
*And as she sings, Ba lilly wean,*
*Little ken I, my bairns father,*
*Far less the land that he steps in.*

*Then in steps he to her bed fit,*
*And a gromly guest I'm sure was he,*
*Sang Here am I, thy bairns father,*
*Although I be not comely.*

*I am a man upon the land,*
*And I am a silkie in the sea.*
*And when I'm far and far from land,*
*My home it is in Sule Skerry.*

*Ah, tis not well, the maiden cried,*
*Ah, tis not well, alas cried she,*
*That the Great Silkie from Sule Skerry,*
*Should have come and brought a bairn to me.*

*Then he has taken a purse of gold,*
*And he has laid it on her knee,*
*Saying, git to me, my little young son,*
*And take me up thy nourris-fee.*

*It shall come to pass on a summer's day,*
*When the sun shines hot on every stone,*

*That I shall take my little young son,*
*And teach him for to swim the foam.*

*And thou shalt marry a proud gunner,*
*And a proud gunner I'm sure he'll be,*
*And the very first shot that ever he'll shoot,*
*he'll kill both my young son and me.*

*Alas, Alas, the maiden cried,*
*This weary fate's been laid for me,*
*And then she said and then she said,*
*I'll bury me in Sule Skerry.*

This heart-rending story portrays the wheel of fortune. Ballads are songs or poems depicting vulnerability in the world. They represent the grief of humanity.

## Welsh Seal Lore

The story of the selchie circles the Isle of Albion to Wales in a story told in the fourth of the *Four Branches of the Mabinogi*, about Math, Son of Mathonwy. Math tests Arianrhod for her purity. From this test is born Dylan ail Don, translating to Dylan second wave, who is the first-born son. Arianrhod is the mother aspect of the Welsh triple goddess. In the *Mabinogion*, she is the daughter of Don, and the sister of Gwydion and Gilfaethwy, and eventually gives birth to two sons, Dylan ail Don and Llew Llaw, who were both conceived by a supernatural process. The selchie legend of Wales tells the tale of how Dylan was born. Preceding Dylan's birth, he was baptised and thereafter submerged himself into the ocean and transformed into a selchie. He became forever free in the spirit of the ocean.

## Irish Seal Lore

Seals were honoured in ancient Ireland, and are seen as powerful and potentially threatening to humans, especially fishermen around the coastal regions who made their living from the sea. One story shares of a time when St Brigid entertained guests at her home in Ireland. Brigid asked a local fisherman if they could catch a fish for her guests who would later dine with her, but the story goes on to say that the fisherman instead harpooned a seal. But whilst he did this, he was pulled into the ocean. The seal dragged him in the water all the way to shore on Britain. When the rope finally broke free, the man was left stranded upon a rock. But luck was with him, as he eventually made it home. Before he did, he went in search of the seal, who was resting on the shore of Leinster, caught it, and sent it home to St Brigid to share with her guests.

Evidence relating to the highly developed relationship between human and seal in Ireland is shared in the words from James Hardiman (ed.) (1846) *A Chronological Description of West or H-Iar Connaught, Written A.D. 1684,* by Roderic O'Flaherty.

*Many traditions, connecting these harmless animals with the marvellous, are related along our western shores. Among these there is one of a curious nature, that at some distant period of time, several of the Clan Conneelys (Mac Conghaile), an old family of Iar-Connaught, were, by 'Art magick', metamorphosed into seals! In some places the story has its believers, who would no more kill a seal, or eat of a slaughtered one, than they would of a human Conneely. It is related as a fact, that this ridiculous story has caused several of the clan to change their name to Conolly.*

# Seal Lore of Norway

Tales of the selchie can be found around Scandinavia. John MacAulay, Gaelic historian, and author of *Seal-folk and Ocean Paddlers: Sliochd nan Ron*, believes the seal folk were people who came from Northern Scandinavia in sealskin-covered kayaks, and landed on Scottish shores. John upholds his beliefs that many of the folk who live in the Western Isles of Scotland are descended from *Sliochd nan Ron* – seal people – and these people were the Sea Sami of northwest Norway. The nomadic Sami tribes of Northern European peninsula dressed in seal pelts, and the theories about the Sami being the seal folk is a contemporary interpretation.

Humans have hunted pinnipeds for thousands of years. Evidence shows that Canada has hunted the ringed seal for over 4,000 years. Today seals are hunted commercially in six countries: Greenland, Iceland, Norway, Canada, Russia, and Namibia. Scandinavia is split into two groups of Sami – the Sea Sami, who were fishermen, skilled at hunting, journeying great lengths in kayaks made of seal skin; and the Mountain Sami, who were the reindeer herders who nomadically migrated with their reindeer between summer and winter pasture lands. The Sea Sami do not hunt the seal anymore; they only hunt fish. Sea Sami culture is alive in respect of mythology, clothing, music, and fishing, but they have lost their traditional relationship to the seal.

The Sea Sami used seal skins to make their kayaks, but the skins would only remain dry for a certain amount of time. The kayakers would then have to come ashore, take off their sealskin coats and clothes – probably wearing nothing underneath – to let them dry out in the sun's penetrating warmth. Imagine passing by and noticing this act, and how it resembles the selchie maiden story of the lady shedding her skin.

How on earth did the Sea Sami navigate treacherous north seas and high waves, travelling miles to a different continent, where waves frequently rise to eight feet high, regardless of storm force oceanic flow? How did they sail through such sea weather? John M MacAulay states: "...where the kayaker enters an oncoming wave, or dives completely from sight, indicate the ability to submerge the kayak as will." John continues to say, "The kayak is completely decked over, apart from an opening, or manhole, which varies in shape and size, generally no larger than necessary to accept the occupant whose upper clothing is fitted to the rim of flange of the manhole to make a perfectly watertight seal." John quotes W. C. Scouter, "the man and the kayak become one."

Yet there are theories that a kayak made of seal skins could not withstand long water voyages, as these skins become waterlogged and loose buoyancy. If this is the case, how did the Sea Sami cope on long haul trips? As John further writes:

*It would be quite inappropriate to furnish an easy solution to the age-old mystery of our seal folk and visitation by strange people in kayaks, to rob future generations of the intrigue and the delight of flirtation with the unknown would be to discharge too recklessly our vast treasure house of folklore.*

So, whether or not John's theory has grounding, the myths and legends of the selchie were spoken about and continue to enchant our hearts today. Around the same time that the Sea Sami culture and their seal hunting faded into history, Gaelic culture and the stories of the selchie ceased to appear on Scottish shores.

In Norway, seals are magically under the spell of the Norwegian King, so the saying goes. From his book, *Superstitions of the Highlands and Islands of Scotland*, John Gregorson Campbell (page 283/284) writes:

*It is a popular saying that seals and swans are 'king's children under enchantments' (clann sigh fo gheasaibh). On lonely mountain meres, where the presence of man is seldom seen, swans have been observed putting off their coverings (cochull) and assuming their proper shape of beautiful princesses in their endeavours to free themselves from the spells. This, however, is impossible till the magician, who imposed them, takes them away, and the princesses are obliged to resume their coverings again. The expressive countenance and intelligence of the seal, the readiness with which it can be domesticated, and the attachment which, as a pet, it shows to man, have not unnaturally led to stories of its being a form assumed by, or assigned to, some higher intelligence from choice or by compulsion.*

This idea relates to the story of the selchie maiden told on North Uist, the Outer Hebrides, and relates to the Outer Hebrides having a strong connection to Norway in bygone days.

John Gregorson Campbell shares his knowledge about a story of seals being injured, and a tale with Scottish fishermen who travelled to Norway. It has the same theme as the story from *Tobar an Dualchais*, "Shetland taboo against killing a seal."

*These are persons, a native of these northern islands writes (in a private letter), who come across from Norway to Shetland in the shape of large seals. A Shetlander on his way to the fishing, early in the morning, came across a large seal lying asleep on a rock. Creeping quietly up he managed to stab it with his knife. The animal was only slightly wounded and floundered into the water, taking the knife along with it. Sometime afterwards the fisherman went, with others, to Norway to buy wood. In the first house he entered he saw his own big knife stuck up under a beam. He gave himself up for lost, but the Norwegian took down the knife and gave it back to him, telling him never again to disturb a poor sea-animal taking its rest.* (John Gregorson Campbell, *Superstitions of the Highlands and Islands of Scotland*, page 283/284.)

# Seal Lore of Canada

The further north of the world we travel, we encounter the Inuit cultures of Canada. Seals are a protected species in the British Isles. The indigenous people of northern Canada depend on their traditional hunts, as it provides food and clothing to the Arctic peoples, who have no other source of nourishment. Inuit hunters have great respect for the spirit of the seal, as they are not just a practical source for them, but it represents a way of life. In bygone days, life for the Inuit would not have been possible without the seal. The Netsilik Inuit who reside in the Canadian Arctic are called *the People of the Seal*. There is a great deal for us to learn from the indigenous cultures of the world, their simplistic ways of living, communicating, and respecting the land and its animals, and their practical knowledge. Traditional Inuit spirituality lives in contemporary hearts, even though many Inuit today have Christian beliefs.

Archaeologists found that the First Nations People in Canada, and the Inuit of the Arctic Circle in Greenland, Russia, and Alaska, have been hunting pinnipeds for the past 4,000 years. Their meat provides humans with protein, vitamin B12, Vitamin A, iron, and essential fats. All the seal is honoured, and the velvet soft pelts are used for clothing. They are revered in Inuit legends, Inuit place names, and as a form of spiritual reference. The Netsilingmiut also called *the people of the seal*, live in northern Canada. An Inuit hunter's method of spearing and capturing a seal is to lie flat with their face on the snow, then crawl along the ground in a set of movements that impersonate the seal. The seal is a sentient being – gentle, enchanting, with soft silky fur, but they too are killers; they hunt to survive just as the Inuit do.

Seal hunting is a tradition the Inuk have carried out for centuries. There are no plants in the Arctic and pinnipeds are a part of the staple diet. The documentary 'Angry Inuk', produced in 2017, shares how the people in Iqaluit – the Capital of Nunavut in the Canadian Arctic – and their community have been nurtured and survived by seal hunting – not culling. Ethically hunting seals, with a conscience, they only source what they need, not what they want. Economic options in that region are few, and the selling of seal skins for traditional clothing in extreme weathers in the Arctic is crucial to Inuit communities. Indigenous cultures have hunted pinnipeds for millennia; they do it to feed their families and to avoid starvation.

In the olden days, the Inuit believed in animistic religion where every being has a soul. The angakkut (Inuit medicine people) communed with the spirit world and wore animal carved masks when they wished to communicate with a certain animal in a ceremony. Inuit danced in snow houses during ceremonies with shallow one-sided drums, sang songs to spirit world, and told ancestral stories about the *genius loci*. The Inuit held rituals around hunting by honouring the animals and paying deep respect before and during the hunt. They believed the spirit of the animal killed would be reborn in another animal. Some Inuk placed a small lump of iced water into a departed seals mouth, and this was so all the seals of the ocean would not go thirsty. A potent ritual message to the spirit of all pinnipeds. Even today, individuals in Greenland believe in a symbiotic relationship between human and animal, and when they hunt, they breathe the words *"thank you"* into the spirit of the seal they have killed.

As David F. Pelly mentions in his book, *Sacred hunt: a portrait of the relationship between seals and Inuit*:

> *Traditionally, the hunt is the pact between Inuit and the seal. The Inuit hunter is not extracting from the environment but creating a bond between his people and their environment. When the seal gives itself to the hunter, it is an act of sharing in which the seal is transformed from animal to human. Being consumed is a form*

*of rebirth or renewal for the seal. According to ancient Inuit philosophy, sharing among all beings makes survival in the Arctic possible.*

Inuit means "people". The Inuit weave legends of the Tunit – a mysterious ancient people that once inhabited their lands – and the gods and goddesses who protect their snow-filled lands. One of the most important goddesses in Inuit culture is Sedna, known as Nuliajuk or Taluliyuk. Sedna is mother of the sea, who lives within the Arctic oceans, and takes care of all oceanic creatures. Sedna symbolises the seal. In the beginning, Sedna disagreed with her father, and for punishment he denied her from returning home, banishing her to the ocean. As Sedna held onto the kayak which she had been cast out upon, her father chopped off her fingers so that she would let go and be forever lost. But this only turned the forlorn girl into a sea creature that resembled the seal. Her fingers magically turned into whales and seals the Inuit hunt. Time passed by, and Sedna's courage and fortitude grew. She became sovereign over the oceans and seas. The pinniped is a significant messenger for her people.

The late James Archibald Houston, author of *Treasury of Inuit Legends* who was disillusioned with urban life, spent twelve years living and travelling in the Canadian Arctic, among the Inuit peoples. Accomplished in art, he was called Saumik, the "left-handed one", by the Inuit. James shares his first-hand experience of the Inuit mythology, and a song passed down by the elders to the young.

*Once, on south Baffin Island, I saw this myth come alive. Some young children were playing near a tidal ice barrier with many dangerous hidden cracks. Their grandmother crept with great care down among the ice hummocks and from a hidden position called out, 'Oohhwee, Oohhwee!' The children ran back onto the land and said the sea goddess Taluliyuk had frightened them. Later, the grandmother said, 'I told them about the woman who lives under the sea. Now she will keep them away from the dangerous places.' The grandmother was referring to the powerful sea goddess in this central Arctic song.*

*That woman down there beneath the sea,*
*She wants to hide the seals from us.*
*These hunters in the dance house,*
*They cannot mend matters.*
*They cannot mend matters.*
*Into the spirit world*
*Will go I,*
*Where no humans dwell.*
*Set matters right will I.*
*Set matters right will I.*

(Houston, James. The Goddess of the Sea: The Story of Sedna. The Canadian Encyclopedia, *23 April 2015,* Historica Canada.)

Hougharry graveyard, hamlet of Hougharry,
Isle of Uist, Outer Hebrides, Scotland.

Hougharry graveyard, hamlet of Hougharry,
Isle of Uist, Outer Hebrides, Scotland.

The ancient part of Hougharry graveyard,
hamlet of Hougharry, Isle of Uist, Outer Hebrides, Scotland.

Seal viewing point, Isle of Berneray,
North Uist, Outer Hebrides, Scotland.

The Selchie's Grave, Olrig, Caithness, Scotland. *Robyn Jobson.*

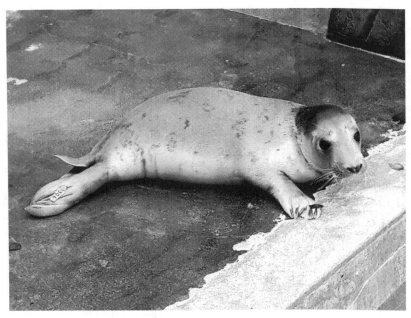

Elizabeth, the Cornish Seal Sanctuary, Gweek, Cornwall, 2017.

Elizabeth the Celtic seal's release, Porthtowan,
Cornwall, 18th December, 2017.

# Part II

# The Magic of the Seal

The resting place of the seal. "I possess neither land nor sea, therefore I am free," whispered the seal, "fear not liminality, but embrace the threshold as you accompany me through the Otherworlds of transition – dance in it, as feathers dance in a breeze." Seals have zero control over their environment, and they are liminal creatures. In anthropological terms, liminality is a rite of passage. It stems from a Latin word *limen*, translating as "a threshold." In a metaphorical sense the magic of the seal takes us on a journey of trusting liminal space. From land, into the sea they go, repeating this act over and over, and sharing with us that it's safe to walk through a precipice of change. There are many times when liminality crosses our paths, as we transition through life from age to age, and year to year, as we change jobs, move dwelling places, outgrow relationships, and experience our loved ones die. Transitioning through a temporary space, one may feel empty, lost, and in limbo, as we prepare for new beginnings. Seals travel through liminality every day. And rest gently, after rather exhausting hunting pursuits, they are nevertheless content and peaceful with their existence. They neither belong entirely to the ocean or land; continually crossing boundaries. To a seal, a temporary space is natural. They are powerful medicine.

The seal ebbs and flows with the moon and the tides. Their connection to the moon is potent. They behold the essence of moon within their hearts, of divine feminine flow and wisdom. The moon is connected to the energy channel within us and runs through the left-hand side of the body towards the brain. In ancient yoga traditions, this is called the *Ida Nadi*. The brain holds life's memory and is integral to the craft of storytelling. The selchie teaches us to come back to our sacred feminine heart of deep intuition, and in their silence, they hold space for reawakening and transformations.

Through storytelling, we reconnect to all of nature. As we dive into the stories of the seal; as we try and understand their intrinsic nature and way they navigate life, our hearts open up to pinnipeds. As we walk the land which has been walked upon for a thousand years, and cross paths with semi-aquatic mammals, our understanding of being in *relationship* with seal expands. The ocean, and the seal, shapes us and brings us home to a place we have drifted so far away from. They find freedom in movement, as they meander, and dash through azure seas. We too can find freedom in oceanic adventures such as wild swimming. With free-flowing movement, we can glide through the crisp, cold ocean just like the seal.

Seals find peace resting on the shoreline; we too can find peace at the ocean side, through stilling our minds and immersing ourselves in presence. As we gaze at the beauty of pebbles and seashells; as we observe the different colours of seaweed; as we feel the icy cold-water rushing over our bare feet; as we feel the sea breeze on our face, and taste sea salt on our lips. We come home to ourselves at the ocean. The seal curiously seeks out oceanic creatures, and play with seaweed and with each other. Although mostly solitary creatures, they do form connections. They are in unity with the land around them, and we too, can form connections with the ocean. We are not so different from seals, as we work, rest, and curiously seek experiences.

If a seal metaphorically chooses to accompany you on life's journey, you are blessed. I feel an affinity with them, not only because of my encounter finding a wild Atlantic grey seal pup, but because they speak to my soul. We all have lessons in life. Certain lessons could be to speak our truth and love ourselves. The selchie maiden story is a reminder to love ourselves first and foremost, as we take back our metaphorical seals' skin, and rekindle our inner child. Adult grey seals are heavily clad by blubber, having up to six centimetres around their belly shielding them from the cold. They are a symbol of protection too.

A belief in seal lore is a thoughtful, reflective, and private kind of spirituality. It is sacred knowledge. The selchie maiden story is about the holy grail of returning to oneself, of finding the secrets of our soul, and the grail within ourselves. Pinnipeds awaken the sea priestess within, as we explore deep into the psyche of our minds to find answers and inner freedom. If it's freedom you seek, freedom is found in creating boundaries. Imagine yourself swaddled in a silver-grey seal skin. This fur gifts you healing, strength, and protection, as you navigate life's challenges. Seals are betwixt worlds, and they bring balance to our lives as they dive from one world to the next in their waking days.

The symbolism of the seal/selchie represents:

Alchemy of one's inner world
Aloofness
Confidence
Courageous when vulnerable
Creativity
Curiosity
Emotional depth
Enchantment
Freedom
Gentleness
Healing
Homecoming
Intelligence
Intuition, and instinct
Joyful, and playful
Liminal space – everything in life is temporary

Magical
Messengers of the afterlife
Otherworldly
Peaceful
Precision
Protection
Psychic senses
Returning to one's true self
Sensitivity
Shapeshifting (acting skills)
Shyness, and timidity
Strength
Transformation

The metaphorical seal skin offers protection, creates boundaries, and is a safe space to heal. Observe their unique traits, and let them appeal to your curiosity. What aspects of the seal do you sense is mirrored within you? Primitive man honoured animals that had imitable traits. Families would call lands, roads, and themselves, after the animal's name and honour it as a family member. There are many places named after seals. Shillay, for example, (Scottish Gaelic: *Siolaigh*) is an island in the Outer Hebrides of Scotland; the name comes from the Norse *selr-oy*, meaning seal island and is the western most Island of *Heisgeir*. Shillay has hundreds of pinnipeds bask on its shores during each pupping season. There is also a place in Sutherland, Northern Scotland, called *Eilean nan Rón* in Scottish Gaelic, known as Isle of the Seals.

*Pinniped*, which means fin-footed in Latin, is a term used for seals. They are said to have evolved from bears, dogs, or otters, and their order name "caniformia" means dog-like. One can differentiate between grey seals and common seals by the shape of their heads; the grey seals are more dog-like, and the common seals have shorter foreheads and are more cat-like. The heads of female grey seals are shorter, and those of male grey seals have lengthier, broader snouts. Males are darker skinned, with less fur patterns, and have an added bulge towards the rear flippers. Female grey seals are lighter, with dark fur patches, pale underbellies, and no protrusion between their retractable nipples and rear flippers. Their whiskers, known as vibrissae, are incredibly sensitive and detect movement from afar. If you notice, their eyes are positioned further apart on their face than those of humans or other animals, and when swimming this gives them a better side view for detecting predators and food sources. They swim on their backs, not through the novelty of relaxing or playfulness, but because they have a greater field of vision upside down.

Seals are as flexible as cats. They twist, turn, and create banana poses when they are trying to keep their sensitive parts out of cold waters, and these poses indicate they are feeling safe. They glide across golden sand on their bellies, in the same motion as a caterpillar, which is called hobbling. In the ocean, they dart around, navigating hunting grounds, swiftly manoeuvring through waters after having shut down their breathing.

*Survival in the open ocean and around our coast is tough, and even helpless-looking seal pups must be born hardy. Huge storms whip our seas into tumultuous peaks and deep abysses. Breakers relentlessly pound our shores, energised by gigantic Atlantic swells, sometimes for weeks on end. Low tides provide some respite, but at high tide most seals are forced to take their chances at sea.* (Sue Sayer, *Seal Secrets: Cornwall and the Isles of Scilly*).

Seals make a conscious decision to dive, and fifteen seconds before they go under the water, they pull blood from their periphery into their core and slow their heart rate down. A seal's heart rate decreases from 120 beats per minute to 5 beats per minute, which shuts down their circulation, and they dive between 10 to 30 minutes with each breath hold, without starving their brains of oxygen. Seals, in contrast to humans, breathe out before swimming to empty their lungs of oxygen, and this allows them to stay underwater for an incredible amount of time. If they get caught deep in the ocean and are stuck for oxygen, they have emergency oxygen supplies in their spleen. Seals crush their own spleen to pump oxygen out, which in turn replenishes their supplies and allows them enough time to resurface. Pinnipeds have extra ribs that protect their lungs, and when they dive their ribcage collapses due to them having a floating sternum. This floating sternum, with connective tissue to their ribcage, enables their ribcage to collapse under pressure and is a part of their evolving adaptation which increases their hunting efficiency. Humans, in contrast, have a fixed sternum. Life is a consistent challenge for seals, yet they continue to thrive every single day.

Pinnipeds feed almost entirely on ground and benthic fish, but indulge on lobster, crab, eels, mackerel, octopus, and squid. They swim slowly, and mostly near the seabed. As fish swim, they leave a hydro dynamic trail in the water, just as a boat does, and whilst gliding through the sea, seals locate fish by picking up this vibrational trail from over 100 meters away, using their extraordinarily sensitive whiskers. One day, my brother was diving off the west coast of Cornwall, when he found a rock crevice with a large edible crab in it. Andrew peered into the cave to look deeper, and as he did, a grey seal swam behind him and pulled on his rubber diving fin with its teeth. A little shocked, Andrew gazed in awe at this semi aquatic being as its inquisitive eyes stared at him. My brother decided to peep into the crab cave once more, and again, the seal tugged his diving fin. This happened three times. The incessant pinniped was politely telling him it was her crab, and was not to be touched by human hands.

Another time, my brother dived off the local slipway. Whilst he was looking at two spider crabs deep underwater, another grey seal come up to him. Again, it pulled on his flipper. I believe she was telling him not to touch the crustaceans, for they were her friends – or later dinner. Seals devour crustaceans, and eat according to the variety of fish abundant to the season. Andrew recalled the seal swam next to him for a long while and at one point floated right in front of him, and stared into his eyes. Andrew said he couldn't stop smiling because of the encounter.

There are many endearing stories of how seals interact with humans, and if you happen to cross paths with one, it may curiously swim up to you. Remain calm and refrain from approaching it yourself, but allow it to investigate you of its own free will. A seal's safe place is in the ocean, where they are most powerful. Notice when they are on the rocks, they move *gently* into the water to acclimatise their bodies. They are one of nature's most curious creatures, and their inbuilt resilience has kept their species alive for centuries.

## Meditation to connect to the spirit of a seal

Learn to speak the language of the seals and bring their messages back from the ocean. To connect to the sacred heart of the seal, we must first connect to our own heart, recognising the spark of magic residing within us. Place your hand up to your heart, and breathe into this space of infinite love, and psychic sensibilities. Take your time as you feel into your magical heart space.

This meditation will take you on a journey to the depths of the sapphire oceans where you can connect to a seal, or a selchie. Not all seals are selchies; it's usually the larger grey seals that behold the selchie spirit. Remember, there are thirty-three individual breeds of pinnipeds around the world, and any one of these may wish to individually connect with you in meditation.

The seal who wishes to connect with you will have individual markings – light or dark grey fur. They may be a pup adorned in white lanugo fur; they could be an unusual ribbon seal with two stripey colours of grey and brown, or black; or a rare albino seal, or an all-black melanistic seal. Whoever greets you will be your spirit companion.

Connecting with their essence in journeying will take you safely to the depths of your soul. They may wish to share with you something about your true natures that you are not embodying, or a part of yourself you may have forgotten about. And they will bring you back safely to land, to grounding and stability, as you integrate the meditation experience.

*Bring your mind into the present moment.*

*Close your eyes, feel the earth beneath you, the sky above you, and the air around you.*

*Relax yourself and take some deep breaths, letting go of any thoughts from your day. Gently breathe in and out, and relax further.*

*Continue to breathe deeply and feel yourself go deeper into a state of relaxation.*

*Let the silence of the day pleasantly embrace you.*

*Imagine a spark of light within you, and allow that light to expand outwards from where you are sitting, all around you. Then expand that light to the ocean.*

*See yourself sitting in a quaint rowing boat, on a calm ocean, close to a remote Scottish island.*

*You notice a dolphin swims to the side of the boat and greets you.*

*You sit on the side of the boat and get ready to immerse yourself into the water. With the dolphin by your side, you both submerse yourselves in the waters.*

*You swim deeper and deeper with the dolphin to guide you, and the azure waters soothe your spirit.*

*As you reach the bottom of the ocean, you stop swimming and free float upright.*

*A whirlpool of sand slowly develops in front of you and the ocean becomes misty.*

*Eventually the dust settles, and out of the whirlpool swims your seal companion. You greet each other as if you have known each other before.*

*What does the seal look like? What breed are they? Are they male or female?*

*Does the seal have a name? (Trust the first name that you receive. The name may appear to you later in the day).*

*Is there any guidance the seal wishes to share with you?*

*Does the seal have any knowledge about their world?*

*Does the seal come with a symbol, a song, or a gift for you?*

*Swim with each other, as you get to know about their life.*

*Continue getting to know this semi-aquatic mammal.*

*Take as much time as you wish (5–10 minutes in silence).*

*It is now time to bid your new friend, the seal, goodbye. They look at you with compassion-filled eyes, and you know that you can connect with them at any time in the future. The bond between you is strong and eternal.*

*The dolphin returns to your side, and steadily they guide you to the surface of the ocean.*

*You thank your dolphin friend for being your guide on this journey, as they nudge you with the tip of their nose then joyfully swim off into the distance, leaving you next to the boat.*

*You get back on the boat and row safely back to the shoreline, which is only a short distance away. Upon landing on the shore, you jump out of the boat and pull it inland. You rest on the sand for a while in gratitude for the journey to meet the seal.*

Bring yourself back to the present moment. Shake your hands, feet, and body, and have a glass of water or a cup of tea and biscuit to ground yourself.

# The Spirit of the Ocean

Three realms meet at the sea. As you stand at the ocean's edge, with the sand beneath you, fresh air around you, and the ocean gently lapping over your feet, you are standing within three realms together. If you visit the beach at dawn or twilight, then you add another threshold of liminality. The seals dwell within these spaces every day. They are living in this triad space, which makes them truly enchanting and Otherworldly. To understand the magic of the seal is to recognise the magic within the sea, for the ocean is a part of the seal and they spend up to two-thirds of their life out at sea.

As poet Persis Karim wrote, "Go find the place where sky and water meet in the exquisite dance of light and shadow, and tell me you are not slayed by beauty." This is the place where you will find seals. The ocean soothes our sense of self, and in its silence, we can hear ourselves think. The ocean allows us the space to be exactly who we are, as she does not judge. We encounter our raw vulnerability at the ocean's edge and find ourselves as an embodiment of the wild.

The sea is our great mother and the mother of the majestic moon, and contains some of the most mysterious creatures on earth, who all carry individual wisdom. There is a subtle energy in seaweed, in the shells, in starfish, in the dolphins, and whales. Sea gods were considered the most powerful gods. Ocean Nymphs, Sea Maidens, Sirens, are all types of sea fayeries, along with mermaids, and selchies. Manannan Mac Lir rules over the Otherworld, and his daughter Chlíodhna of the Tuatha Dé Danann is the Celtic goddess of the afterlife, and embodies eternal love, enchanting beauty, and endless healing. Manannan protected the Sidhe as they were defeated by the Milesians, on the plain of Tailtiu. By magic, Manannan summoned an enchanted mist, which granted the sidhe a cloak of invisibility from mortal eyes and guided them into their new kingdom in the Otherworld.

The ocean is a place where you can journey in your imagination across, or under, to places of the Otherworld. It is a place of the afterlife, where spirits, and the sea-people, all reside; it is the place of everlasting life. In ancient myths and legends, journeys to the Otherworld were taken by a person going into a trance-like state induced by drumming, meditation, and generally by connecting to nature in depth. The telling of stories, poems, and reciting words were all ways of accessing the Otherworld.

The ocean's water is ancient, created at the beginning of time. It is a primal source where life began and where one day we may return too. The seal dives into the ocean, and an Otherworldly essence every day, and this action could be a metaphor for us accessing our subconscious minds. Anyone can access the Otherworld of insight, and imagination; it is not limited to only those who have the two sights. The Otherworld contains symbolism, and insightful teachings, through our sixth sense and imaginations.

When you go walking on remote beaches, you may feel an Otherworldly sense in the spirit of the place, and you may not feel alone as you sit in silence at the ocean's edge. This spiritual essence is predominantly so on the Inner and Outer Hebrides islands in Scotland, and at places like the Achill Island, County Mayo in Ireland. Gently meditate at these places to feel into the *genius loci*.

As you journey around the coastline, you may find yourself drawn to a certain body of water which resonates with you more than another. For me, the Sound of Harris, and the sea channel by the Outer Hebrides sings to my heart the most. It is called the Minch, (*an Cuan Sgitheanach*), also called the North Minch, and the Lower Minch, (*an Cuan Canach*), also called the Little Minch. For hours, I watched seals at play in these waters. They are truly contented in their lands of origin. And I feel a deep remembering there, which I don't feel at the Atlantic Ocean on the north coast of Cornwall, which is where I live.

The North Sea is another body of ocean that stirs a sacred heart connection within me. The darkness of the North Sea can feel a little unnerving, yet I feel at home investigating its depths, especially on the crossing from Aberdeen to Orkney. You, too, may feel a sacred connection to a certain sea. Which waters calls to you the most, and why is that so?

Around 230 miles east of the island of North Uist, in the Outer Hebrides, beholds a mysterious rock of basalt form. This rock protrudes from the Northern Atlantic Ocean. James Fisher, a British scientist, claimed the island to be "the most isolated small rock in the oceans of the world." It is believed to be the summit of a long-lost volcano site, which exists around 65 feet from the ocean floor. There are theories that Rockall may be the last remaining piece of land which formed the lost continent of Atlantis.

If this is true, is it any wonder the Selchies and spirit of mermaids gather around the Outer Hebridean islands closest to Rockall, where the original stories of half animal, half human beings from Atlantis were created?

*As well as two kinds of fairies, there seems to be two kinds of mer-folk in the Hebrides, one being some of the Fallen Angels who took refuge in the sea and in whose veins runs not blood but living fire, and the other, more ordinary, mermaids who often marry mortals. These seem sometimes to be half human, half sea-creature with a fish tail in place of feet, and sometimes to be the people of lost Atlantis who, although resembling the ordinary mer-folk in most ways, are of a higher type of civilization and intelligence and possess the gift of prophecy. (Otta Flora Swire, The Inner Hebrides, and their Legends.)*

It has been said that the ancient sea fayerie are attracted to the frequencies of Atlantis, but the legend of Atlantis is based on theories and speculation. There is a lot we will never truly understand about the world of the Selchie; they remain one of the most mysterious sea fayerie of all.

Land has a positive effect on the mind, body, and spirit, but so too can the sea soothe our mind and help us transition through a therapeutic healing journey, whichever method of therapy we embark on. We can wild swim, surf, bodyboard, paddleboard, scuba dive, duck dive, and play in the waves; letting our anxiety fall away as we become one with the ocean. The ocean is not judgemental. It allows us to be fully ourselves, it is a mirror to whatever we hold inside, and is a place where we can let go of restricted emotions. And you will be left with a feeling of lightness and freedom. The seals must feel this exuberance every single day.

My father and brother are both scuba divers, and I learnt from an early age to respect the ocean. I understood it is far greater than me, and I will never truly win against it in a match. So, I honour it. My father told me an ancient proverb, "Time and tide wait for no man." The origin of this saying is not known, but the earliest record was from St Mather in the year 1225, *"And te tide and te time pat tu iboren were, schal beon iblescet,"* Its meaning is that we have no control over the tide, nor the ocean's flow.

As a young girl, I vividly remember standing at the ocean's edge, sensing it's not only our intuition we need to trust, but also our wits. Therefore, we need to navigate the ocean, learn the rip currents and when it's safest to swim, and where not to go. We need to read the ocean, as a psychic reads tea leaves, studying the winds, the tides, the geography, the sea creatures that live within it, just as the seal does. The magic of the seal encourages us to connect with the spirit of the ocean, where we can find our true selves' wisdom, again and again.

## Ocean Treasures

Water is ancient. By connecting to the ocean's gifts, you are connecting to our first mother. You can meditate with sea treasures on the beach and note your findings in a special sea journal, or take photographs and meditate with them later. Our ancestors have traded and used seaweed in their diets for millennia, and archaeologists have found seaweed at ancient settlements in the British Isles. As an ocean vegetable, it's invaluable for our health. Taurine is found in the red algae and shellfish, and fish is beneficial to the brain. Iodine found especially in brown seaweed is beneficial to the central nervous system, by synthesising the thyroid hormones.

Dulse seaweed is mentioned in the seal stories, like 'The Silkie Painter' when Mary visits the shoreline to collect dulse, and seaweed is mentioned in 'Fair Maids Tresses' by Duncan Williamson in *Land of The Seal People*. In the 17th century, dulse was used in Scotland for medicine to cure hangovers and scurvy. Seaweed has been used as a healing tool many years.

It has been said it helped humans become who we are today, as our humanity is defined by our brain development, and seaweed encourages brain health. The oldest green seaweeds found fossilized in rocks were discovered by palaeontologists, dating back to 800 million years. The British Isles is home to over 600 species of seaweed alone, and it plays a large part in the marine ecosystem. Seals do not specifically eat seaweed, yet they are known to play with it! One day, I sat for half an hour watching a juvenile seal pup play with seaweed, and my heart sang with joy. It was hilarious watching him flick it up in the air for it to then land on his head. They eat sea creatures, molluscs and fish, and crustaceans eat algae-eating plankton, so they receive its benefits that way.

The British Isles is home to Celtic seaweeds such as kelp and wracks. Common types are bladder, knotted, spiral, and serrated wrack, gutweed, oarweed, sea lettuce, sugar kelp, and purple laver. The ocean will envelop you with its wisdom in its own time, but these lessons are not to be rushed, just as peace is not to be found; it is to be experienced.

Seashells are fascinating in their own right, and scatter shorelines around the British Isles. Each individual shell has a story to share. They include the auger shell, baltic tellin, banded wedge shell, common cockle, common limpet, common oyster, common periwinkle, and muscle shells. Shells connect you to the divine healer within you.

The ocean embodies everything in her heart; she is a healer, a gift-giver, yet she also takes away. The ocean holds humanity's consciousness from the beginning of time, until the end of time.

## Meditation to connect to the spirit of the ocean

The animal, plant, tree, and stones all have a subtle energy; so too do the creatures of the sea. The ocean is powerful, and she beholds sea beings who have something special to teach you about yourself and of the magic of the sea. Here is a meditation to meet an ocean creature. This could be a seal, a selchie, a fish, starfish, a crab, dolphin, lobster, octopus, whale, walrus.

*Firstly, relax yourself, and gently close your eyes.*

*Ground yourself by imagining you are connected to the earth.*

*Take some deep breaths and let go of all your thoughts from the day.*

*Feel the power of your breath move through you, then bring your mind into the present moment.*

*Continue to breathe deeply and feel your body go deeper, and deeper, into a state of tranquillity.*

*See yourself sitting on a quiet beach; you are looking out towards the ocean, with the waves gently lapping over the sand.*

*Next to you lies a large grey seal; she is gazing at you with wonder.*

*In a sensitive way, the grey seal flaps her flipper and communicates to you. She flops on her belly and heads towards the ocean, ushering* you to follow her, and you both head out into the water. The waves lap up against you as you go further out into the sea.

The seal turns to you again, her eyes beaming with pure love. She asks you to trust her, and you reach for her flipper; as you do, she dives into the ocean, at great strength of speed, taking you deeper and deeper until you reach the ocean floor. Miraculously you can breathe under the water, and you feel safe with her as your guide and companion.

As you stand in amazement at being under the water, all of the sea creatures pass you by – the fish, the starfish, the octopus, the jellyfish, and even dolphins gather. They start swimming together in a large circle, and this encourages the sand to make a whirlwind. You see the vortex of sand but cannot see through it. Gradually, this whirlwind comes towards you and gently begins to lose its power. The sand starts to gently fall back to the seabed, and from beyond the whirlwind is an ocean creature who wishes to teach you something. This ocean creature, or sea elemental, moves towards you.

What do they look like?

Do they have a name? (Trust the first name that is given to you).

Is there any wisdom they wish to share with you?

Do they present you with a symbol, a word, or a specific colour?

Look at where they come from, and how is it different from your world?

Continue getting to know your companion.

Go swimming with them, or rest on the seabed as you learn about their life.

Take as long as you need (5–10 minutes in silence).

Gently give thanks to the ocean creature for visiting you, and bid them farewell.

As you look towards your left, you see the silvery-grey seal companion waiting for you.

She swims by your side, and with her loving eyes, ushers you to take hold of her flipper.

*She leads you to the ocean's surface and with you by her side, gently swims ashore.*

*She flops onto the beach in a caterpillar movement, and you both move towards the place where you began your journey.*

*Resting next to each other on the sand, you gaze out towards the ocean.*

*You thank your seal friend for being a guide on your journey to the bottom of the ocean.*

*You gently open your eyes and come back into the present moment.*

*Leave a biodegradable and honourable offering to the ocean as thanks.*

Connecting to the ocean can send us deep, into an unknowing feeling, and we need to be gentle with ourselves coming out of a relaxed state of mind. Because the sea is not a human's natural environment, you may feel more spaced out after coming out of a meditation with the ocean. So, make sure you ground yourself properly. Use grounding exercises – have a hug, pet an animal, stand by a tree, have a drink of water, a cup of tea, and eat something wholesome – chocolate and biscuits included!

A note: When gifting a sacred offering to the ocean and the seals, make sure it is a biodegradable, honourable offering, such as a song, a poem, a pinch of herb, sea salt, the shake of a rattle, the beat of a drum. You could even collect a small bottle of water from the ocean, take this water home, place it on the seal altar, pray over it for the healing of sea creatures, and take the healing water to pour back into the ocean. Another sacred way of gifting would be to pick up litter on the shoreline. Bless the ocean, who is your first mother.

### Ideas to connect to the spirit of the ocean

As we explore the seal's natural environment, "leave no trace". Honour coastal treasures by leaving rocks, wildlife fauna, flora, and natural objects as you found them.

- Beach Cleans – spend time collecting rubbish washed up by the sea and dispose of it in a responsible place.
- Create sand art, labyrinths, mandalas, and build sandcastles. Use watercolours, or acrylics and paint the ocean in all of its vibrant colours.
- Dance on the beach and imagine the spirit of the seal dancing with you. Let your arms flow freely at the tide's edge.
- Discover individual seashells!
- Enjoy water sports – surfing, bodyboarding, kayaking, paddleboarding, scuba diving, and snorkelling.
- Explore rockpools – responsibly and with awareness. If you witness a fish or crab, make sure to act with care and leave the sea creatures alone, or place them *gently* back where they came from.
- Explore the geology around the coastline near where you live. What types of sea stones scatter the shoreline?
- Listen to the sounds of the ocean.
- Meditate and relax – spend time being still at the ocean's edge to restore your inner peace.
- Pray at the ocean's edge. Offer prayers and blessings to the *genius loci* of the sea, the people of the sea, and the seals.
- Take photographs of special ocean findings.
- Watch the wildlife come and go from the coastline. There is an array of ocean creatures and sea birds to discover; you may even see a seal swim by.
- Wave jump – connect with your inner child and have fun playing with the ocean's waves.
- Wild swim.

# Songs from the Shoreline

Scientists praise seals for their great intelligence and their astounding connection to humans. As they are known to be fond of music, scientists have studied how they copy human voices and sing, and how seals' vocalisations adapt when imitating songs. The old tales speak of the seals' power of communication, and how they conversed in the oldest Gaelic language.

Have you ever heard a seal cry out? It is similar to a human's cry. Seals are beyond our understanding of intelligence; they know things we never will. In the book *The Inner Hebrides and their Legends* by Otta Flora Swire, Otta remarks that:

> *Seals love music and will listen by the hour to bagpipes or songs. It is said that occasionally, though rarely, the seals themselves sing and that when they do it is so beautiful a sound but so terrible in its sadness that those humans who have heard it can bear early life no longer but plunge into the sea to join the seals. Others say seals sing only as a death call or a warning.*

Seals communicate with grunts, barks, and loud moans, and they convey messages by slapping their bellies when feeling threatened and to warn trespassers to stay back. Their sound is loud and often quite shocking; they sound human-like. Otta says:

> *But in Iona it was thought that they come together and sing for joy only when one of their numbers has extirpated his or her sins and attained salvation and that as the song is a song of perfect, unselfish joy in the Mercy of God, it is the music of Heaven, which no man can hear and live. St Columba certainly cared for the seals.*

The old stories were embedded in animistic beliefs of how seals spoke to people and how people spoke to seals as a deep connection took place. But not everyone could understand their words, as they spoke in the oldest form of Gaelic which not many could comprehend. They have been singing songs since the beginning of their existence, yet humans have forgotten how to listen.

In the anthology *Sailormen and Servingmaids. The Folk Songs of Britain Volume 6* (Caedmon 1961; Topic 1970), the booklet states:

> *In the west of Scotland, where seals abound, there are many tales of their response to human contact. I've been told again and again of seals that raised their heads out of grey, curling waves, to listen as long as anyone would sing to them. That this is not superstition is confirmed by a contemporary account of an American woman, who made a pet of a seal and swam with it all one summer. The seal would wait in the surf for her every day and call out to her as she came down the cliff to the beach.*

In the selchie legends, when seals transform into human, they speak in old Gaelic. In the book, *The Peat Fire Flame* by Alasdair Alpin MacGregor, he says:

> *Those of you who have read the Dan nan Ron, the Song of the Seals, will recall how Manus MacCodrum, himself one of the seal-folk, would be knowing when the tide was ebbing across the great Reef of Berneray — how he would hear the call of the skua on the rocky promontory, and the wailing of the moon-restless plover on the hill behind — how, after the earthing of his love, and the tide had ebbed in his heart, he would be crossing the Sound of Berneray continually and making for the old Pictish tower known as Dun Sticir in the shadow of Beann Bhreac — how the island folks would be seeing him at low tide upon the Reef of Berneray, singing wild and strange runes.*

This story speaks about the MacCodrum Clan who are descendants of the seal people.

The seals' power of speech and interaction with humans have been spoken about throughout time. In an account from Stiofán Ó hEalaoire, a renowned storyteller from County Clare in Ireland, he spoke of a seal pleading with fishermen to save her life. There was a boat on the ocean with many fishing nets, and as the fishermen drew the nets back in, a seal was entangled in them. The fishermen heard her cry, "I am not a Conneely or a Joyce! But it is far from my family I have sailed!" The fishermen did not pull up their lines any further, and let the seal go free. This tale speaks about kinship between human and seal, of how their cries stirred sympathy in the hearts of fishermen.

Over the years, seals have been heard mourning their lost loved ones. Far out at sea, they have also been known to guide fishermen out of danger from rocks; fishermen hear their cries and avoid the rock. Chanting, drumming, singing songs of healing, are ways of gifting back vibrationally to the ocean and the pinnipeds. When I stand at the ocean in my local Cornish Bay area, I send prayers to all the sea creatures.

There is one song written by Harold Boulton, called "Song of the Seals", which has been sung on the Hebrides Islands since 1935. It attracted a host of seals who gathered around and listened longingly to the singing, and the chorus is like a chant in itself. It indicates seal calling has been performed throughout the years. These songs were used to charm the seals, and although it is not wise to disturb any semi-aquatic mammals whilst they are resting or sleeping, I could imagine in bygone days it once being sung at the ocean's edge.

## Song of the Seals
*A sea maid sings on yonder reef,*
*The spell-bound seals draw near;*

*Her lilt that lures beyond belief*
*Mortals enchanted hear.*

*Hoiran, oiran, oiran, oiro,*
*Hoiran, oiran, oiran, eero,*
*Hoiran, oiran, oiran, eelaleuran,*
*Hoiran, oiran, oiran, eero.*

*The wond'ring ploughman halts his plough,*
*The maid her milking stays,*
*While sheep on hillside, birds on bough,*
*Pause and listen in amaze.*

*Was it a dream, were all asleep,*
*Or did she cease her strain?*
*For the seals with a splash dive into the deep*
*And the world goes on again,*
*But lingers the refrain.*

Below is a ballad called "Song of the Sea" by Tomm Moore, who directed and co-produced the enchanting, animated film, *Song of the Sea*. This song is worded both in English and Irish Gaelic and is filled with liminal magic.

Between in and between out
*Idir ann is idir as*
Between north and between south
*Idir thuaidh is idir theas*
Between west and between east
*Idir thiar is idir thoir*
Between time and between space
*Idir am is idir ait*
From the shell

*As an sliogan*
A song from the sea
*Amhran na farraige*
Neither quiet nor calm
*Suaimhneach na ciuin*
Searching fiercely for
*Ag cuardu go damanta*
My love
*Ma ghra*
I am between love
*Ta me idir ghra.*

Song of the Sea © 2014 – Cartoon Saloon – Melusine Productions – The Big Farm – Superprod – Norlum. All rights reserved.

Take yourself back in time, and imagine our ancestors sat on the ocean side calling to the seals, waiting patiently for them to heed the invite. *The Seal Summer* written by Nina Warner Hooke shares an old Celtic seal call.

**Celtic seal call**
*I call you, my brother,*
*I call you by your home name, which you know well.*
*If you hear me, come without fear.*
*The tide runs strongly. The water is so cold.*
*I am waiting and watching.*
*Come to me.*

Songs for the seals have been sung in times past. Now, it's time to create your own Celtic sea songs, as you travel the coastlines and hum the melodies at the shoreline and pray for all semi-aquatic mammals. Sing your blessings to the ocean and the seals, and sing blessings to your soul as you remember your heritage and soul's strength. All the while, remember to keep a safe and comfortable distance from all resting seals, so as not to wake or cause them to look at you and move. In some cases, mothers abandon their pups if disturbed. It is vital to bear this in mind.

# Seal Altar

Create an altar of purpose in honour of the seals. An altar serves as a focal point and will increase your connection to this magical being. It is a centre point for the focus of healing, and a bridge to yourself and the seals. The spirit of the ocean will bestow a magic on your altar, where you can focus on your love of pinnipeds and contemplate what they mean to you. It is a place where you can pray for the protection of the seals. A place of pure consciousness, where you can become closer to the spirit of the seal.

As we dwell in prayer for Mother Ocean and the thousands of individual seals who roam free, we are inviting peace into our own lives. I often think of Elizabeth whilst in prayer; my seal mother's heart lingers in a place of pure love. Prayer centres me and give me a sense of belonging, helping me to feel a part of the greater whole. Prayer induces a sense of homecoming, and in being transformed by acts of love, we become more inspired with life.

Find a clear and quiet spot in your home to create a seal altar which you can decorate with coloured cloth, blue, and white candles, and sacred sea objects. Purify the space by saining (blessing) it with Celtic herbs, sprinkle holy well water, sea water, or by saying a prayer. Saining is a Gaelic tradition of purifying space. The Gaelic art of saining could include using a small branch of rowan tree to sprinkle ocean water or holy well water to bless the seals, your home, and loved ones. Rowan, St John's Wort, Juniper, and Yarrow can be burned, but if you are handpicking these from nature, remember to collect them in a sacred manner and leave an offering to the spirit of the plant.

In bygone days, women tended to the waters of life and used water in baptisms, blessings, anointing, and dowsing; waters connected them to the feminine mysteries. The ocean is our great mother and is also mother to the moon. Seals carry the essence of moon energies as they ebb and flow with the tides, and the eight phases of the moon: the new moon; the waxing crescent moon; the first quarter moon; the waxing gibbous moon; the full moon; the waning gibbous moon; the third quarter moon; and finally, the waning crescent moon. The moon moves both the ocean and the seal in their everyday lives. Pinnipeds understand the way of water.

Assemble your altar as simply or extravagantly as you wish. Give offerings to the altar throughout the days and weeks, and remember the most potent offering you could ever give is your heart and prayers. Hospitality, to the Gaels, was seen as a sacred offering. A warm-hearted welcome was given when a stranger came knocking, and this kindness can still be felt on the islands of Scotland. Give offerings to each other and to those who are in need of help, as this shows respect and strengthens the community spirit.

My seal altar is simple, with a few shells, a porcelain selchie figurine, and a painted shell from Berneray. Spinner and weaver Michaela Cordes created a Celtic silver-grey seal skin prayer shawl, spun in Scottish wool, and blessed by sacred waters from Iona. This prayer shawl kept me warm during the winter months and offered me a sacred space to heal, and to connect to the seal. As I did so, inspiration flowed. During the winter storms, seals suffer adversity, as they battle the stormy waters, so I spent time in prayer for the seals, and Elizabeth. I worry, as a *seal mother's* heart does. I use the term seal mother in a metaphorical sense, of course.

Light a candle in prayer for all the pinnipeds of the world. Write a poem or story for all the seals. Create your own prayer as I have below.

## The Seal's Prayer

*Great mother ocean, hear my prayer for the seals,*
*Deep within the centre of the sea,*
*May peacefulness become you, oh seal of peace,*
*May an abundance of fish be yours*
*May you be free from man's carelessness, and disturbance*
*Mother sea, grant all seals protection, and strength,*
*And in strength, courage to overcome challenges,*
*As you endure the test of time,*
*I honour you, seal,*
*My kindred, my ancestor, my heart*
*Great mother ocean, thank you for hearing my prayer.*
**Melanie Godfrey**

# The Healing Power of Seals

The night before I began writing this chapter, I dreamt I was taken underwater, and with a calm heart, I began breathing as naturally as breathing air. I swam in an aquamarine essence; fluorescent-green seaweed floated by my sight; the water was so clear. Unafraid, I viewed the oceanic life set out before me. My dream deviated, and I saw myself with a silver-grey skin covering my whole body, and all the while I stood in a snow-white hut built by Inuit. As I fell into a trance, I began dancing, and the seal skin and its head became a part of me. I experienced sensory feelings of being taken fully into the world of the seal. The dream faded, and I awoke.

Seals have danced alongside humans for the indigenous people, whose shamanic and animistic beliefs have existed for thousands of years. Medicine people and shamans of indigenous societies not only feed themselves from seals, but allow a deeper connection to bring about wisdom and healing. For the costal Sami people of Northern Norway, the Inuit of Northern Canada, Iceland, the people of Greenland, Finland, and the Faroe Islands, they were the most predominant natural resource for oil, food, and clothing.

Spirit Healer, or shaman, or saman, is a term used by the Tungus of Siberia who dance with spirit world to bring back messages of soul loss and healing to their communities, and medicine people cure disease through traditional methods. Sacred stones, trees, and the animals' spirits were said to be able to interact with people. In indigenous culture, animals, ritual, and livelihood are interlinked. Animals and mammals, including semi-aquatic seals, were a key concept in Inuit shamanic practice, and animals were said to watch over the shaman and guide the practitioner. It was an Otherworldly experience.

In a study of the Siberian Eskimos, Tassan S. Tein states that "Shamans of the patriclans played a large role in the conduct of social affairs" (Tein 1994). Unappointed but influential, the Angakoq led and participated in ceremonies to appease the great spirits of the sea and sky. He also influenced personal lifestyle choices of villagers by keeping watch over the maintenance of cultural taboos which might anger the spirits.

*For instance, during the closing performances of the Traditional Bladder Festival, the shaman climbed out through the skylight to enter the sea, visit the seal spirits in their underwater home, and request their return.* (Fienup-Riordan 1990.)

If the spirits were not pleased with the way that the Inuit had upheld their taboos, people might become ill, food might become scarce, or bad weather might plague the village. The Angakoq would have to bargain with the spirits to compensate for the misdeeds of the villagers and bring harmony to the balance between nature and man. Mayer, Lauren (2004) "Sami Noaidi and Inuit Angakoq: Traditional Shamanic Role and Practices."

Edith Turner, a distinguished anthropologist and author, who worked among the Inupiat of Northern Alaska, tells a tale of when she met with a whaling man and seer, and of how the spirit power of the seal is a large part of Inupiat culture.

*I listened in wonder to a story given by Clem, a whaling man, and a seer. (I have changed people's names to preserve their privacy.) It was the story of a sick man whose spirit was failing. In this story, it was the seals that healed. It may seem strange that healing should come from humble animals, but it was highly meaningful from the Iñupiat point of view.*

*Clem said, 'A man was very sick. When he was about to die, he found himself traveling under the sea ice to the underwater house of the seals. When he came to the door of the seal house, he went in by the double porch, the place where people take off their parkas and hang them on pegs.'* Clem then pointed to his own double porch where rows of parkas were hanging.

He continued, *'The clothes hanging on the pegs in the seal's double porch were all sealskins. The man went inside. He thought he was going to find seals without their skins, but no, they were people. Underneath their skins, the seals were people, sitting around in a circle. One of them had very long ears. This was the seal-person who could hear everything that went on in the village – you've heard of the Long-Eared One.'*

*The seal people took the man in, and he stayed with them for a whole year, learning shamanism. At the end of the year, the seal people showed him the way back under the ice to his house and said goodbye. He came to himself in his bed, quite well, and found he'd only been away from home for one hour.*

*This kind of experience has happened to others. The soul sometimes travels when in extreme danger – and in our culture, we have heard of the near-death experience. Also, the story attests to the fact that wisdom or skills may be imparted in one great event.*

*One begins to understand why the Iñupiat hold seals in reverence. In this ice-bound environment, hunters are continuously among wild animals, and they are dependent on the generosity and self-sacrifice of animals in order to exist. Thus, the spirit power of the animals looms large, especially those of seals, whales, and eagles.*

(Turner, Edith. "Shamanism and Spirit", *Expedition Magazine* 46.1 (2004): pp12–15. *Expedition Magazine.* Philadelphia, PA: Penn Museum, 2004.)

# Safety at the Ocean

The sea can soothe our souls, yet it can also be unpredictable and treacherous, offering no mercy. Seafarers have great respect for the sea. The ocean is vast, and only certain parts are navigable, familiar, and have currents, like flowing rivers, that work in favour of the boats which cross their path. It's wise to know how to keep yourself safe when you visit the ocean, as even in calm waters there can be hidden rip currents. Seals naturally know how to read the ocean, but to humans, the sea can be foreign.

- In the United Kingdom, in an emergency at the ocean call 999, or 112 for the coastguard.
- Check the tide times so you do not get cut off. The ocean moves quickly and is deceiving.
- If you find yourself in danger whilst in the ocean, float – floating can help you to survive.
- Let someone know which beach you are going to if you are going alone.
- Respect the ocean; it saves lives.
- Take note of beach signs and flags, as they warn of dangers and rip tides. Rip currents are difficult to discern, even by experienced beach dwellers. They can be identified as a channel of water which looks choppy on the surface while the rest of the ocean is calmer; the water can churn, making the water murky looking. If in doubt, ask a lifeguard or experienced swimmer's advice, and swim on a lifeguarded beach for extra safety.
- Tides rise and fall from each day to the next. Each tide is unique with spring tides, high tides, low tides, and neap tides. Check weather forecasts at the www.metoffice.gov.uk, and tide times at www.tidetimes.org.uk.

- Trust your intuition at the beach; if it doesn't feel right, then don't put yourself in unnecessary danger.
- When walking on any cliffs, stay away from the edge, and avoid walking on cliffs in high winds. Take note of any danger signs which may indicate possible rock fall. Stay safe, however adventurous you feel.

# Protecting Wild Seals

William Wordsworth so beautifully expressed, "nature never betrayed the heart that loved her." This is one of the many hidden meanings behind seal lore, and maybe if seals could openly speak, they may insist, "observe me, but nay disturb me, for I am the one who shapeshifts at twilight, through shadows of resurrection. It is me, seal, wandering the spirit veil, between spaces where magic is real!"

Seal disturbance is a real issue affecting *pinnipeds* today. Seals wait patiently for their favourite rocks to become available at low tide, where they spend time in relaxation. Yet they can easily be disturbed, as they notice, hear, and smell humans, as if on high alert. So, to prevent seals from the fear and worry of interference, always stay a safe 100 metres away from any that are resting. They are solitary by nature, only spending time with other pinnipeds when they haul-out, and this is for safety reasons.

It is also not wise to share the named location of any seal haul-out or pupping sites online, as people will flock to them and cause possible disturbance. Use a generic, vague name instead. Protecting wild seals is an act of love.

In the book *The Devil and the Deep Blue Sea: An Investigation into the Scapegoating of Canadas Grey Seal*, Linda Pannozzo explains how seals have long been scapegoats of the sea, and how they can help to increase the fish populations that we enjoy, because they feed on the predators, and rivals of the fish we don't necessarily enjoy. Within aquaculture, salmon farmers in Scotland face problems with seals. Fishermen don't wish to hurt them, but as they are natural predators and hunt fish, seals get entangled in fishing nets and this is a constant worry. Seals can be a nuisance to fisheries and fishermen, but that does not give them any less right to be there. Properly tensioned and maintained anti predator nets around fish farms are known to effectively protect farmed fish from seals. Protecting wild seals today is a far cry from the seal culls which took place throughout history, and in 1978 when culls took place in Scotland, specifically around Orkney, it resulted in a collective outcry. Luckily, the public voice was heard and there have been no official seal culls in Britain since.

The Atlantic grey seal has over time been an ethical and environmental issue, with the mental and physical state of seals coming under scrutiny in animal welfare groups. In understanding large mammal populations and to assist the environment to create balance and harmony, there is a fine line between intervening with natural ecosystems and the damage this can cause. When protecting seals, humanity reassesses its changing relationship and bonds to the natural world. Seals are ocean messengers; they bring back information about the vast pollution and inhabitable sea conditions, and as I said before, we need seals as much as they need us in the fragile cycle of life. As top predators, they are vital in helping keep marine ecosystems in balance. Thriving seals, mean thriving fish and thriving fisheries.

## How you can be of service to the seals

When you go walking on beaches, take a bag to collect rubbish, plastic, or discarded nylon fishing nets that you encounter and dispose of them in a safe manner. Fishing nets are one of the main causes of injury and death in seal population, as they get entangled because they play with the nets. When they are caught, they spin to try and free themselves, thus entangling themselves even more. Cut looped items so they do not get caught around seals' heads.

Do not feed seals as this encourages connection to humans, causing lifetime changes to their natural behaviours and putting them in danger. In spite of how much they may beg – practise tough love.

Harm no seal. It is a criminal offence to take, injure, or kill a seal, as they are a protected species in the British Isles. The grey seal (*Halichoerus grypus*, a Latin name meaning hook-nosed sea pig) and common seal (*Phoca vitulina*, a Latin name meaning calf-like seal) are native to Celtic seas.

Human activity is playing havoc with marine life. Seals and cetaceans become stranded and often harmed by fishing activity. Injury takes place from boat propellers, unsustainable fishing practices, and seals are hurt from discarded fishing gear. Noise from wind farms disorientates certain species of marine animals. The ocean is stressed by pollution, and the warming of the oceans. The future of fishing and coastal activity needs evaluating.

If you find an injured seal, do not approach it, but contact British Divers Marine Life Rescue, a seal rescue or wildlife centre and wait for them to arrive. Seals can bite, similar to how a bear bites, and wounds can become infected.

If you find an abandoned seal pup, if needs be, stand in-between the ocean and the pup to avoid it escaping into the sea where it may perish, and drown until it has shed its white fur, which may take a few weeks. *Never* encourage a white fur seal pup to go into the sea. Observe the pup from a distance over a period of time, and if the mother does not return, it is likely it has been abandoned. Report the information to a helpline about the seals condition, rolls of skin or hipbones if visible, its size, possible injuries, and the state of ocean and weather. Keep calm to avoid stressing the baby seal.

Choose accredited wildlife safe operator boat trips https://www.wisescheme.org/.

Keep dogs on a lead when seals are nearby.

Remember that seals haul out of the ocean for different reasons to:

breed

digest food

moult

rest to replenish oxygen levels

restore energy from foraging at sea

socialise

thermoregulate (maintain core internal temperatures).

## It can be a criminal offence to disturb seals in protected areas

Report injured, abandoned, or dead seals to the local British Divers Marine Life Rescue, or the RSPCA (Telephone Numbers in the back of the book).

Become a volunteer for a local seal group to help them gather data from seal and wildlife sightings. The data collected will be sent to the government which in turn supports the protection of coastal areas and creates protected sites. Contact the Seal Alliance to discover your local seal group www.sealalliance.org.

Respect seal lore told to us by traditional oral storytellers, for these stories teach us how to honour nature and seals.

Seal Disturbance is one great threat to the pinniped population today. Disturbance is interpreted as a change in a wild animal's behaviour as a consequence of human interaction, which can disturb a seal's vital resting time. Disturbance looks like heightened awareness in the seal's mannerisms, a general look of discomfort. Seals will move towards the water by stampeding over boulders which could injure their bodies. Injuries include ripped-out claws, belly gashes, and broken bones, and sometimes results in death. Pregnant seals could injure their unborn pups, and pups may be crushed as the adults' rush to safety. It is key we all work towards avoiding seal disturbance.

## Actions to prevent seal disturbance

- Be considerate and refrain from taking selfies with seals or their pups. Pups have been abandoned by their mothers as a result of people getting too close. Seals need *safe spaces* to just be. Protect their safety and space. Leave them in peace.
- Be quiet and whisper.
- Keep a distance and low profile (recommended distance is 100m+).
- Refrain from using drones around individual seals, and large haul-out sites.
- Stay low and downwind.
- Use binoculars, telescopes, and cameras with zoom lenses to watch the seals from afar.
- Seals sleep in water, which is called *bottling*. As they fall asleep, they sink under the water's surface. Oxygen levels decrease from the seal's body. Then, as if by magic, a natural reflex is activated in the flipper to propel the seal back to the surface of the water. All of this takes place whilst they are sleeping. Although seals can sleep perfectly well in and under the water, they sleep better on land, as it gives their brains a better opportunity to properly shut down and where they do not have to worry about predators and ocean currents.
- Share information about seals; awareness can save a seal's life.
- Support local seal sanctuaries.

# Elizabeth the Celtic Seal

I will start this chapter with *once upon a time,* although this is not a fairy-tale but a true story of a heart that fell head over heels in love with a wild grey Atlantic seal. Elizabeth is no selchie; she is enchanting, with her own exquisite fur patterns, unique designs that beautify all seals along with their own characters and personalities.

It was a misty autumn evening in the quaint hamlet of Boscastle on the 10th September, 2017. I planned a last stroll along the cobbled pathway towards the coastal path, where I would peer over the ocean's horizon and thank the day for its gifts. After that, I would head back to my bed to read some more, then sleep.

But destiny had a plan that night. An hour before my walk, I had been reading at the youth hostel, the light rain fell from the sky, and night drew closer. My soul felt still as I listened to the trickling of water from the River Valency – a sacred meeting place where river water meets sea water, and where magic occurs. I felt compelled to go for a last walk around the quaint harbour, so with a kind of urgency, I left. It was getting dark, yet I felt the spirit of the sea call me. I reached the headland point to look out over the Atlantic. There were few people around, and the atmosphere felt tranquil.

Dusk arrived, so I walked back along the harbour's edge. The sea was treacherous that night, as a storm had been in force all day. Glancing into the harbour water, I saw a tiny white seal. Mesmerised by her presence, I watched for a long while before realising she was distressed and trying to land. I later learned that grey Atlantic seal pups' white fur, known as lanugo, is not waterproof. The fur becomes saturated and the animal can drown, so they need to be land-based for the first weeks of their lives. Common seal pups are different in that they can swim safely as soon as they are born.

The ocean offered no compassion; the tide was high and gave no place for the pup to land. But *something* must have been guiding her, and as she peered up at me, I ushered her with my hands to swim towards the slipway where she could find safety. As I guided her around the harbour's edge, she tried to climb the harbour walls towards me. Eventually, realising she could land on the slipway, she flopped on the cobbled stone.

I hurried down to her, wary in case her mother was close, and aware I should not touch any wildlife. Seals are protected by the Marine Mammal Protection Act, whereby it is against the law to touch, harass, or feed a seal, so the rule is to always keep a safe distance. Yet this little girl was in big trouble, and time was of the essence.

A passerby helped me pick her up and carry her far enough up the cobbled path to get out of the water, where she would be safe from the storm. But the lady left quickly, as it was getting dark, and before she did, she stressed, "Look after the baby."

I contemplated what to do. It had gone seven o'clock and the rescue places were closed, but I found a number that was answering. The rescue service told me they could not come out as it was too late. I explained the pup needed help and asked what would happen if I left her and she fell back into the ocean. Would she die? The rescue people replied, "There is a possibility that may happen."

I gazed at the helpless lump of fluff lying next to me. "I will stay with her until you send someone out then," I decided, "even if it means me watching her overnight." The administrator took my number and I put the phone down. Resigned to the fact that I would be here for a while, I huddled in my jacket. I looked around for a place to put the pup where she would be safe, but there was nowhere. The tide reached high up the harbour slipway; the waters were trepid on the other side of the harbour wall. If I left her, she would either roll or hobble back into the sea, and I knew it would take her life.

I sat on the harbour's edge with the pup resting on my leg. Her wee nose was scuffed and slightly bloodstained from where she had been crawling up the harbour walls. The sun went down quickly, and the darkness of night descended upon the earth. The light rain continued to fall from the blackened skies.

I said a prayer to help and protect her, and I imagined golden light streaming over her tiny body. I had been with the pup for over an hour and her mother was nowhere to be seen, so I made a promise I would not leave her. As her fur dried, it became as soft as white down feathers. Utterly exhausted, she lay next to me, eyes closed tight, and there she slept. I fell in love – a love that lasts to this day. The wee seal was only three or four days old, separated from its mother, malnourished, and weighing only 12kg.

Unsure of how much time had passed, my phone rang, and it was the British Divers Marine Life Rescue people, who reassured me they could get to us both in an hour. A sense of relief washed over me. Yet that hour seemed to last forever. Sitting in pitch black at the end of the harbour, I could see lights in the distance and the seal's white fur lit me up. All the while she slept.

The dark was consuming, and at first the rescue people could not find me. I waved my mobile phone light in the air and heard them draw closer. In the short time I spent with the gentle pup, I connected with her soul. I felt responsible for her safety. I felt a moment of being a *seal mother*. The rescue people arrived, and we gazed at the vulnerable pup. "Take care of her," I whispered.

Arriving back at the youth hostel, a woman who was staying there met me with concern. "I saw you go out and not return," she said, "and I got worried."

"I had found a seal pup and had to wait with her."

Shocked, she gasped, "Is it in the shower?" My hands had suggested I'd brought the pup back to the hostel.

Hastily I replied, "No, the Marine Divers Rescue came to help her. She will be on her way to the Cornish Seal Sanctuary now."

## The Cornish Seal Sanctuary

Sleep eluded me that night, as the wee pup was on my mind. Would she last the night? I put out a prayer request via social media, and I prayed, too. I kept in contact with the rescue people, and they told me she had been taken to the Cornish Seal Sanctuary hospital site, where she was being fed fish soup! However, she was not out of trouble just yet. It was a week before the pup stabilised, but I went to visit her and saw her slowly recover from her ordeal. I often wondered if I had done the right thing, intervening with nature, but I could not have let her fall back into the high tide where she would have met a dreadful fate.

Most male seals never breed, spend all their lives alone, and are quite happy to do that. It is only the beach masters who mate, and are bright and patient with their girlfriends. Seals communicate through intricate body language. The females stay pregnant for eleven months of the year and can pup right throughout their lives. Initially, there is a strong bond between mother and pup, but grey seal mothers leave their pups to fend for themselves as early as three to four weeks old. The mothers do not feed whilst nursing their pups, and have to rely on blubber for nutrition. So, although it seems harsh, she has to leave them to feed, otherwise she will not survive herself. Seal pups then fast for around one to four weeks and shed their lanugo fur to become waterproof before heading out to sea. "Over 50 per cent of seal pups die each year before reaching the age of six weeks. These are natural deaths." (Ken Jones, *Seal*

*Doctor: The delightful story of Ken Jones and his orphan seals*). The early months of life for pups are harsh.

Seal pups develop teeth before they are born, but teeth will not have formed if they are premature. Luckily, Elizabeth was not premature so had a higher chance of survival. Scientists have found that Weddell seal pups in Antarctica are born with enormous brains, around 70% as large as their mother's, as opposed to human babies who are born with brains around 25% the size of their mother's. This phenomenon enables seal pups to have complex skills and reach self-reliance sooner. I imagine grey Atlantic seal pup brains are similarly formed, as they are fully functioning at only three weeks old, and individual pups have been known to swim as far as 1000 kilometres and routinely dive to 120 meters before they are twelve weeks old.

That autumn, there was a *Poldark* theme for naming the seal pups at the sanctuary. There was none fairer than Elizabeth Warleggan in *Poldark* – the regal lady of Trenwith House – and this pup was so gentle, vulnerable, and extraordinarily beautiful that I named her *Elizabeth*. The volunteers at the seal sanctuary reported back that she lived up to her namesake and was a real diva, being unusually vocal for a wee pup, and that she was an extremely pretty seal.

On 1st October, 2017, she was transferred to the outdoor nursery pool with another pup named Jewell. This was the next stage of her rehabilitation and where she would learn how to compete for fish. On the 10th October, 2017, she was moved into the convalescent pool, where she would spend time with other rehabilitating seal pups.

Each week I visited the sanctuary to see Elizabeth's progress, and my *seal mother's* heart overflowed with love. I noticed her do tiny somersaults in the water; she would flip over and it was like she was dancing. Joyful in her spirit, transparent in her happiness, she was surrounded by playmates and a constant flow of fish food. It was the highlight of my autumn visiting

Elizabeth, and I became passionate about the wonder of seals. They are thoroughly enchanting, and behold an otherworldly magic I had not noticed until then.

One day, I stood at the poolside and prayed for Elizabeth to "be a brave girl and find an abundance of fish to eat so that you will grow up big and strong." Two months later, I received a call from the sanctuary to let me know Elizabeth would be one of the first seals to be released back into the wild, because she was the weightiest pup residing there. Perhaps my prayers truly had been heard. In essence, I had become a *seal mother*, worrying and fussing over this little soul. And even today, I continue to care deeply for all of the seal kingdom.

## Released back to the Wild

On the release date of 18th December 2017, Elizabeth – along with Drake, Dwight, Rosie, Neptune, Prudie, and Jewell – were released back into the wild at Porthtowan beach, in Cornwall. Once near the ocean, Elizabeth turned around one last time and gazed at me before hobbling into the sea. I watched her swim into the distance until I saw her no more, and then I realised I may never see her again.

It would now be very different for her; there would be no free fish or fish soup, and she would have to hunt as adult seals do. For a while I had pangs of seal mother love, helplessly wondering if she would be safe. One night I dreamt we were together underwater, her seal paw touching my hand. We meandered through salty seas and she taught me to breathe underwater. I remember it vividly. I sang the song of the sea that my soul understands.

When the wild Atlantic storms engulfed the West County's coastal regions during the first winter of her release, I prayed. And my prayers were answered when a year later I received an email saying she had been sighted five times at a secret location on West Cornwall's beaches on 26th April, 2018, the

12<sup>th</sup> November, 2018, the 20<sup>th</sup> December, 2018, and the 7<sup>th</sup> and the 21<sup>st</sup> March, 2019. I received a photograph of her resting, replenishing oxygen supplies, her tag number 304 still attached to her flipper – although she can be identified by her individual fur patterns, also known as pelage, which are akin to human finger prints. Elizabeth has not been spotted since, but there is no cause for concern because she could have gone to pup on another shore. Seals from Cornwall have been known to travel over 1000km and visit four other countries as they explore the oceans.

The British Isles is home to half the world's population of grey seals, who spend two-thirds of their life at sea. They can live up to 30 years in the wild, and a Shetland seal is known to be forty-six years old. Here's hoping Elizabeth has a long-lived life too.

# Conclusion

*As to the seals themselves, no scientific study can dissolve their mystery. Land animals may play their roles in legend, but none, not even the hare, has such a dream-like effect on the human mind: and so, though many creatures share with them a place in our unconscious mind, a part in ancient narrative, the seal legend is unique.* (David Thompson, *The People of the Sea*)

There is never a truer word spoken about seals and their traditional stories. In the course of weaving this book into reality, I sat for hours looking out over the ocean, waiting in anticipation for a seal to pass by, or to witness one at rest. I tried to *think like a seal*. During the midst of writing, I experienced a dark night of the soul, where the ice of winter momentarily gripped my heart and a shadow eclipsed me. I believe this was a teaching of the seal who allowed me to dive into the abyss of my soul, wrapping me in the warmth and beauty of their metaphorical seal skin.

In a way, I had reached a point in my life's journey where I truly was ready to meet the magic of the seal, and for them to guide me on a journey into my subconscious thoughts. But for a long while, I did not get it, because it required intense work, accessing uncomfortable feelings I wished never existed. The seal and its lessons are as deep as the ocean itself. They embody peace, joy, and serenity – all the things we reclaim after surrendering to the fact that we cannot escape our true selves.

I am unable to avoid my vulnerability and the painful parts of my history. Memories wash over me in an ocean in turmoil. I cannot hide from my inner world, just as the ocean cannot hide from the storm, but thereafter calm arrives, and peace and hope reign once again as I learn to trust the process of life for perhaps the very first time. And as the seal travels deeply, oh so deeply into the ocean, they teach us to travel into our subconscious thoughts to heal and to know it's okay to carry both the darkness and light inside. I never wanted to admit to the darkness that was beneath my rose-tinted glasses, or to ever speak of those people who put me in darkness by stealing my beautiful, silvery-grey seal skin of freedom. As a sacred talisman for the therapeutic process, the seal with its silky soft fur is priceless in its mystical, symbolic meaning.

Every time a seal looks you in the eyes, it's like they are willing you to journey with them to the Otherworld of your soul, to dive with them into the waters of trust, baring all, knowing you will be safe wherever they lead you. As with all animals and semi-aquatic mammals, there is sincerity and truth in their eyes, and they will lead you to your own truth, of who you really are. With their flipper in your hand, in trust, you both journey until you find the freedom you may search for. Thank you, oh, thank you, dear seals of the sea, for your lessons, and ancient wisdom.

Exploring the magic of the seals did not inspire meaning in my life, it gave me "experience of life", as Joseph Campbell states, "we feel the rapture of being alive"; experiences of our own reality, and of what we instinctively know within us. I experienced a profound inner peace and understanding of our Scottish Gaelic culture when visiting the island of North Uist. I experienced contentment whilst in solitude at the ocean side, watching seals for hours upon end and where I understood it is about feeling their essence, not capturing it. I experienced wonderment as I pondered their instinctive natures, and I felt a great need to share their story. The seal has given me rich experiences.

I found the spiritual nourishment I crave is right here in the British Isles, quite often on remote Scottish Islands. Our ancestors were rooted in a sacred relationship with seals, and although there will most likely never be a revival of the seals' clans, that does not mean we cannot take seals into our hearts today, hear their voice, and learn to honour them. They are symbolically important to the ancient clans and are true treasures of the British Isles, and with this understanding, I hold them close to my heart, for always.

On that fateful night with Elizabeth the seal pup at Boscastle harbour, I was gifted the encounter of loving a wild animal. You could say I became enchanted, forever taken over by the sea-people, the same as in the story of 'Mary and the Seal' by Duncan Williamson. His story takes place in the Western Isles of Scotland and is about a young girl called Mary, who was the kindliest person. When Mary became a teenager, every evening in the summertime she went off in her father's boat to visit a tiny island in the middle of a sea loch. Time passed by, and the village folk began gossiping about Mary and why she never joined in any of the ceilidhs or took an interest in boys, and her mother became upset and decided to get her husband to follow Mary out to the island one day. When he arrived, he saw Mary playing with a large grey seal, and they were having so much fun together. Mary's mother insisted that her father shoot the seal to protect Mary. She said, "Angus, Mary's enchanted. It's one of the sea-people that's taken over. Your daughter is finished – ruined for ever more. I've heard stories from my grandmother how the sea-people take over a person and take them away for ever more, they're never seen again – she's enchanted." So that is what Mary's father did. He callously shot the seal, and a great sorrow befell him. Mary went out in the little boat to the island, and when she didn't return, her father went looking for her. He discovered the boat on the island, but Mary was nowhere to be seen. As he looked out towards the ocean, he saw two grey seals pop their heads out of the water and they stared straight at him, then vanished under the water. In that moment, he knew he would never see Mary again. (Duncan Williamson, *Tales of the Seal People*).

In truth, I too am enchanted! There is a powerful connection once you encounter a seal, and you will understand if you have ever met one. They move you, and you are forever changed. The magic of the seal led me to visit Otherworldly remote Scottish beaches, whilst seeking stories of our indigenous Celtic ancestors who live close to the wild North Atlantic Ocean, and the seal people. I exhausted my research when looking for information on the Conneely Clan of Connemara, and the MacCodrums of North Uist. I found snippets of information, but never any written evidence of how the seal clans honoured the seal, held ceremony for the seal, or of their deepest thoughts about these semi-aquatic mammals. And even if we did have insight, we could not re-create our ancestors' beliefs in the modern-day world. Perhaps certain aspects of the past are meant to stay hidden, and secret to be held as forever sacred in the mists of time. But what does the seal mean to me now, and what is my interpretation of the seal as a prominent symbol, and sacred being in the 21st century? And how can I serve them in the best way possible?

I imagined myself standing barefoot at the ocean's edge honouring the seals, and when I did my heart expanded in a moment of awe, and a profound serenity washed over me. We live in a rather disillusioned world, people feel ungrounded, lost, and disconnected from their surroundings. It is our job to seek wisdom and find magic once again – that magic which lives inside of us. Once that inspiration is found, we need to go forth and re-enchant the world. John MacAulay, an islander who lived on the Isle of Harris, writes:

> *The seal folk are very real people whom we meet and live within the islands. We can tell who they are and where they come from; but in spite of this there seems to be a cultural deficiency in our attitude to the apparently paranormal – a product of 'civilisation' which prevents us from wholly accepting anything than rational thought*

*processes and substantiated information.* (John M MacAulay, *Seal Folk and Ocean Paddlers: Sliochd nan Ron.*)

Trying to understand the indigenous heritage here on the British Isles, especially the Scottish Gaelic culture, rekindled an inner flame. As the tide ebbs and flows, so too does my connection to my own seal skin. The magic of the seal is more than just a guide; the magic of the seal becomes me. The wisdom in the selchie stories forces us to push past our limiting beliefs of what we cannot be, to become who we truly are. The selchie embodies the holy grail, the mysteries of alchemy and returning. As Theodora Goss so beautifully expressed,

> *It occurred to me that there have always been selkie women: women who did not seem to belong to this world, because they did not fit into prevailing notions of what women were supposed to be. And if you did not fit into those notions, in some sense you weren't a woman. Weren't even quite human. The magical animal woman is, or can be, a metaphor for those sorts of women.*

Metaphorically speaking, I'm the seal. The very core of me is aloof, a little shy, curious, playful, sensitive, Otherworldly, mysterious, peaceful unless provoked. I just want to be left in peace to go about my day, to lead a life of simplicity. The ocean's song is embedded in my psyche, and I return to the shoreline again and again, watching, waiting for the call of the seal to remind me of home. Maybe you too identify with this concept. The magic of enchantment and freedom lives within us all. Each of our journeys is unique, and the seal mirrors individual qualities within us. Now it is time for you to take a journey with the seal and find out what they represent to you.

As I become a voice for the seals in all their sensitive, vulnerable, yet powerful selves, I share only a part of their story. For their story is limitless. You too can become a seal advocate and teach people about the protection of wild pinnipeds. Although they look vulnerable and endearing, we must not forget they are a species that has stood the test of time and evolved over thousands of years. Seals are powerful, with extraordinary swimming skills and a profound ability to hold their breaths for long periods of time. Seals are messengers bringing back valuable information for oceanic research, which helps people to understand and protect the ocean for later generations. They are mirrors of the ocean, and guides to our true nature. Seals are full of magic. And for this reason, I love them so much.

The magic of the seal is eternal, and no matter how much humans strive to understand seals by navigating and perceiving their world both on land and in the sea, with their individual personalities and survival skills. How can we gain a clear insight into the ancient seal clans of West Ireland and North Uist and how they lived their lives beside these semi-aquatic mammals? How did the clans, and our ancient ancestors truly honour the sacred seal? We cannot even begin to comprehend most of these narratives, or the seals' mindset. We receive glimpses into their world which we can cherish and wonder at, but overall, the seals and their legends remain beyond our understanding, and will forever be a mystery.

# Bibliography

*Anthropology, History, and American Indians: Essays in Honor of William Curtis Sturtevant, Totemism Reconsidered,* Raymond D. Fogelson and Robert A. Brightman, William L. Merrill and Ives Goddard who were the Editors. (Washington, D.C: Smithsonian Institution Press, 2002).

Ballard, Linda-May. *Ulster Folklife Journals, Seal Stories and Belief on Rathlin Island* (Ireland: Cultra, Ulster Folk and Transport Museum, 1983).

Bonner, William Nigel. *The Natural History of Seals* (London: Christopher Helm, 1989).

Campbell, John Gregorson. *Superstitions of the Highlands and Islands of Scotland* (Glasgow: James MacLehose and Sons, 1900).

Campbell, John Gregorson. *Clan Traditions and Popular Tales of the Western Highlands and Islands* (London: D. Nutt, first published in 1895).

Campbell, John Lorne. *Hebridean Folk Songs* (Edinburgh: Birlinn, 2018, first published in 1969).

Durkheim, Emile. *The Elementary Forms of Religious Life* (New York: Collier Books, 1961).

Fienup-Riordan, Ann. *Eskimo Essays: Yup'ik Lives and How We See Them.* (New Brunswick, NJ: Rutgers University Press, 1990).

Frazer, James George. *Totemism* (Edinburgh: Adam and Charles Black, 1887).

Freeman, Alexander Martin. *Journal of the Folk Song Society, Irish Folksongs,* 6 No. 24 (1921) 263.

Gomme, George Laurence. *Totemism in Britain* (UK: Read Books, 2010).

Harper, Ken. *In Those Days: Shamans, Spirits and Faith in the Inuit North* (Iqaluit, Nunavut: Inhabit Media Inc 2020).

Harvey, Graham. *Animism: Respecting the Living World* (New York: Columbia University Press, 2020).

Houston, James Archibald. *Treasury of Inuit Legends* (Boston, MA: HMH Books for Young Readers, 2006).

Houston, James Archibald. *The Goddess of the Sea: The Story of Sedna.* The Canadian Encyclopedia (Historica Canada, 23 April 2015).

Hull, Eleanor. *Folklore of the British Isles* (London: Methuen, 1928).

Jones, Ken. *Seal Doctor: The Delightful Story of Ken Jones and His Orphan Seals* (London: Fontana/Collins, 1988).

Lambert, Robert A. *The Grey Seal in Britain: A Twentieth Century History of a Nature Conservation Success.* Environment and History 8, no. 4 (November 2002).

Levi-Strauss, Claude. *Totemism* (London: The Merlin Press Ltd, 1964).

Mac an Tuairneir, Marcas. *Duileach, Elemental* (Dundee, Scotland: Evertype, 2021).

MacAulay, John M. *Seal Folk and Ocean Paddlers* (Cambridgeshire: White Horse Press, 1988).

MacDonald, Archibald. *The Uist Collection: The Poems and Songs of John MacCodrum* (Glasgow: Archibald Sinclair, Celtic Press Publishers, 1894).

MacDonald, Patrick. *The Patrick MacDonald Collection, Highland Vocal Airs* (Highlands Scotland: Taigh na Teud, 2000, first published in 1784).

MacGregor, Alasdair Alpin. *The Peat Fire Flame* (Edinburgh: Moray Press, 1937).

Macleod, Fiona. *The Isle of Dreams* (Portland, Maine: T.B Mosher, 1905).

Matheson, William. *The Songs of John MacCodrum* (Edinburgh: Oliver & Boyd for the Scottish Gaelic Texts Society, 1938).

Moore, Tomm. *Song of the Sea* (Kilkenny, Ireland: Cartoon Saloon, Melusine Productions, The Big Farm, Superprod, Norlum, Film 2014).

Muir, Tom. *The Mermaid Bride and Other Orkney Folk Tales* (Kirkwall, Orkney: Orcadian Ltd, 1998).

Newton, Michael. *A Handbook of the Scottish Gaelic World* (Dublin, Ireland: Four Courts Press Limited, 2000).

O' Flaherty, Roderic. *A Chronological Description of West or H-Iar Connaught, Written A.D. 1684* (Dublin: for the Irish Archaeological Society, 1846).

Pannozzo, Linda. *The Devil and the Deep Blue Sea: An Investigation into the Scapegoating of Canada's Grey Seal* (Nova Scotia, CA: Fernwood Publishing, 2013).

Pelly, David F. *Sacred Hunt: A Portrait of the Relationship Between Seals and Inuit* (Vancouver, B.C: Greystone Books, 2001).

Robertson, Ronald MacDonald. *Selected Highland Folktales* (Exeter, Devon: David & Charles, 1977).

Prebble, John. *The Highland Clearances* (London: Penguin Books, 1969).

Sayer, Sue. *Seal Secrets: Cornwall and the Isles of Scilly* (Redruth, Cornwall: Alison Hodge, 2012).

Swire, Otta Flora. *The Inner Hebrides and their Legends* (London: Collins, 1964).

Tein, Tassan S. "Shamans of the Siberian Eskimos". *Arctic Anthropology*. Vol 31, Issue 1 (1994).

*The Folk Songs of Britain: Sailormen and Servingmaids, Volume 6;* (Caedmon Records 1961).

Thompson, David. *The People of the Sea* (Edinburgh: Canongate Books, 2018, first published in 1954).

Turner, Edith. *The Hands Feel It: Healing and Spirit Presence among a Northern Alaska People* (DeKalb, IL: Northern Illinois University Press, 1996).

Tylor, Edward Burnett. *Primitive Culture* (London: J. Murray, 1871).

Warner Hooke, Nina. *The Seal Summer* (London: Arthur Barker Limited, 1965).

Williamson, Duncan. *Land of the Seal People* (Edinburgh: Birlinn, 2010).

Williamson, Duncan. *Tales of the Seal People: Scottish Folk Tales* (Northampton, Ma: Interlink, 2019).

## Seal and Ocean Conservation Groups

British Divers Marine Life Rescue: www.bdmlr.org.uk

Cornish Seal Sanctuary: www.sealsanctuary.sealifetrust.org

Seal Research Trust: www.cornwallsealgroup.co.uk

Marine Conservation and Enforcement Team: conservation@marinemanagement.org.uk

Marine Conservation Society: www.orcaweb.org.uk

Orkney Seal Rescue: www.helpwildlife.co.uk

Seal Protection Action Group: www.sealaction.org

## Useful Wildlife Contact Numbers:

British Divers Marine Life Rescue Hotline: 01825 765546

Cornish Seal Sanctuary, Gweek, Cornwall, Telephone: 01326 221361

Royal Society for Protection of Cruelty to Animals hotline (England & Wales): 0300 1234 999

RSPCA 0300 1234999

Scottish Society for Protection of Cruelty to Animals hotline (Scotland): 03000 999 999 or 0131 3390111

Report all dead seals to the Cetacean Strandings Investigation Programme: 0800 652 0333 (07979 245893 in Scotland)

Check weather forecasts at www.metoffice.gov.uk and tide times at www.tidetimes.org.uk

"Selkie Moon", by Leanne Ta'lki Anawa.

Three days into my idea about writing a book about seal lore, I had reservations as to whether it was a good idea. I asked to be sent a sign from the universe to see whether I should continue with my research. On the third day, I received an email from a friend who I hadn't heard from in months. Leanne (artist and author of *Lemurian Starchild Oracle*) wrote to me to share a painting she had just completed of the selchies, called "Selkie Moon". The divine synchronicity had me in awe, and I concluded it was a sign to go ahead with writing this book.

# About the Author

Melanie Godfrey was born in Cheshire but grew up in Cornwall, the Land of Saints. Melanie is a qualified Therapeutic Counsellor with the Counselling and Psychotherapeutic Central Awarding Body UK, a Spiritualist Healer with The Healing Trust UK, and currently studying Druidry with the Order of Bards, Ovates, and Druids. She lives in Cornwall, UK.

## You may also like

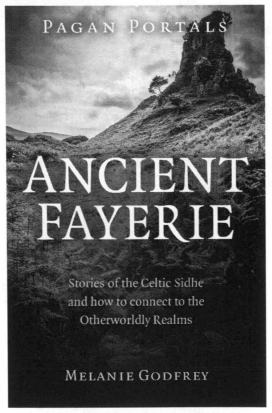

978-1-78279-477-6 (Paperback)
978-1-78279-478-3 (e-book)

## Keeping Her Keys
An Introduction to Hekate's Modern Witchcraft
Cyndi Brannen
*Blending Hekate, witchcraft and personal development*
*together to create a powerful new magickal perspective.*
Paperback: 978-1-78904-075-3 ebook 978-1-78904-076-0

## Journey to the Dark Goddess
How to Return to Your Soul
Jane Meredith
*Discover the powerful secrets of the Dark Goddess*
*and transform your depression, grief and pain*
*into healing and integration.*
Paperback: 978-1-84694-677-6 ebook: 978-1-78099-223-5

## Shamanic Reiki
Expanded Ways of Working with Universal Life Force Energy
Llyn Roberts, Robert Levy
*Shamanism and Reiki are each powerful ways of healing; together,*
*their power multiplies. Shamanic Reiki introduces techniques to*
*help healers and Reiki practitioners tap ancient healing wisdom.*
Paperback: 978-1-84694-037-8 ebook: 978-1-84694-650-9

## Southern Cunning
Folkloric Witchcraft in the American South
Aaron Oberon
*Modern witchcraft with a Southern flair, this book is a*
*journey through the folklore of the American South and*
*a look at the power these stories hold for modern witches.*
Paperback: 978-1-78904-196-5 ebook: 978-1-78904-197-2

Readers of ebooks can buy or view any of these bestsellers by clicking on the live link in the title. Most titles are published in paperback and as an ebook. Paperbacks are available in traditional bookshops. Both print and ebook formats are available online.

Find more titles and sign up to our readers' newsletter
www.collectiveinkbooks.com/paganism

For video content, author interviews and more, please subscribe to our YouTube channel.

## MoonBooksPublishing

Follow us on social media for book news, promotions and more:

## Facebook: Moon Books

## Instagram: @MoonBooksCI

## X: @MoonBooksCI

## TikTok: @MoonBooksCI